I, personally, am so excited over the fact that this road is near final completion that I simply cannot believe it to be true. I am wandering in fairyland. . . Two men, Win Wilson and Wilson Howell, conceived the idea of this road and fostered it. To their everlasting credit let it be said that their every act and thought in the movement has been to advance the health and welfare of the people of Coachella valley.

- Maj. Bartlett Hayes
Comments at the opening ceremonies
of the Pines-to-Palms Highway
June 18, 1932

It took a lot of faith to undertake the building of that road.

-Thorndike C. Jameson
Chairman, Riverside County Board of Supervisors
Comments at the opening ceremonies
of the Pines-to-Palms Highway
June 18, 1932

For Tourism & A Good Night's Sleep

J. Win Wilson, Wilson Howell, and the Beginnings of the Pines-to-Palms Highway

Steve Lech

Copyright © 2012 by Steve Lech
All rights reserved. No part of this book may be reproduced in any form or by any means, electronic or mechanical, including photocopying, without permission in writing.

Published by the author
Riverside, California

Two views along the Pines-to-Palms Highway
(Top) - Leaving Garner Valley
(Bottom) - Overlooking Deep Canyon and the Coachella Valley beyond

Note About Illustrations

All original photographic illustrations are courtesy of the author. Unless otherwise noted, all historic photographs are from the author's personal collection.

Cover illustration map is courtesy of the Automobile Club of Southern California.

Table of Contents

Introduction		viii
A Note on the Pines-to-Palms Highway Name		ix
Acknowledgements		x
1.	Early Travel Between Mountain and Desert	13
2.	Initial Proposals and Construction Efforts	26
3.	Controversy Over the Route	63
4.	Early Construction and More Route Problems	96
5.	Construction by the Federal Government	115
6.	Opening the Road	136

Appendices

A.	Sites Along the Pines-to-Palms Highway	158
B.	"From Pines to Palms"	168
C.	"From Palm to Pine"	175
D.	"From Pines to Palms on the Gordon Trail" & "The 'Pines and Palms Trails' of Wonder"	178
E.	Fulmor's 1921 Report on Palm Canyon Road	185
F.	Fulmor's Report on Pinon Pines Road	187
G.	"Highway May Girdle Mountain . . ."	192
H.	"Pinon Pines Road"	198
I.	"Pinon Pines Route for Mountain Highway Favored by Fulmor"	201
J.	"Celebration of Opening of the Pines-to-Palms Highway"	207
K.	"Fitting Remarks by Chairman B. H. Hayes"	208
L.	"New Highway Over San Jacinto Mountain Area"	211
M.	Where (and What) the Heck was Ribbonwood?	215
	Bibliography	228
	About the Author	230

Introduction

The Pines-to-Palms Highway. The name evokes images of mountain and desert, and the ability to see both in a relatively short period of time on the same road. A part of present-day Highway 74, the Pines-to-Palms Highway is one of the most beautiful and interesting drives in Riverside County. Known for scenic views of the desert, widely varied plant communities, and unique geologic features, it has been an attraction to motorists since it opened in June 1932.

The Pines-to-Palms Highway was born of a desire to unite the desert areas of Riverside County with the San Jacinto and Santa Rosa Mountains. The idea, first conceived in the late 1910s, was brought about for many reasons. First, such a road would allow increased tourism and expansion of tourist-related development throughout both areas. This was vitally important during the 1920s, when the economy of the greater Riverside County area was dependent upon both agriculture and tourism. It must be remembered that during this era, there was a definite "tourist season" throughout Southern California and Riverside County. People came to "winter" in the balmy climate of the region, and continually sought ways to occupy their time. At a time when automobiles were becoming the norm for transportation, it made sense from a tourism perspective for the county to invest in a route that would allow people to see the mountains and desert environments all in the same day and perhaps spend a little money in the meantime. "Aside from the well being of the citizens of Riverside county, the development of the mountains also means the well being of the county treasury. Those rocks and crags, and pines and brooks, can be made to yield shekels of the realm, even as the desert has been made to yield onions and dates," wrote John Winfield (J. Win) Wilson, the unabashedly brazen booster of the Coachella Valley (who, just coincidently, operated the major newspaper there, the Indio *Date Palm*). As we will see, Mr. Wilson played a vital role in advocating the road.

A second reason for a desert-mountain road was that such a road would allow desert dwellers the ability to easily escape the oppressive heat of the summer. In the days before air conditioning, leaving the desert was about the only relief one could find against the heat. Getting to the mountains, though, was not easy, given the modes of travel available to the average resident in the early days. However, by the 1920s, automobiles were becoming the rule, not the exception, and the construction of good auto-accessible roads became a priority to accommodate both residents and tourists alike.

Finally, a road such as the Pines-to-Palms Highway would help to connect back-country areas such as the Cahuilla Valley with larger towns. This too would help open those areas to further agricultural development.

Just what is the Pines-to-Palms Highway? In present-day parlance, it is that section of State Highway 74 from the junction of Highway 243 in Mountain Center to its end at the intersection of Highway 111 in Palm Desert. For the purposes of this book, though, we'll use the historic terminology because it is much easier to rectify with the information available for research. In short, then, the Pines-to-Palms Highway in this work begins at Keen Camp in the mountains, and ends at the Palm Springs-Indio Highway (for a list and explanation of all place names used in this work, please see Appendix A).

A Note on the Pines-to-Palms Highway Name

So many times, one will run across references to the highway as being the "Pines-to-Palms" Highway or the "Palms-to-Pines" Highway. They are seemingly interchangeable due to the frequency of each moniker's use. A myth has even grown up that it is "Pines-to-Palms" if traveling from the mountains to the desert, and "Palms-to-Pines" if vice-versa. However, the true name of the highway is the Pines-to-Palms Highway, as defined by the Riverside County Board of Supervisors on August 11, 1930 – "In the matter of a name for the highway from the San Jacinto Mountains to the desert of Coachella Valley . . . upon motion of Supervisor [John] Shaver, seconded by Supervisor [Harvey] Johnson, and duly carried, it is ordered and determined that the name [of the highway] from San Jacinto Mountains to the Desert be and the same is hereby known as the Pines to Palms Highway." This descriptive name came about due to the fact that the road was constructed from the mountains to the desert. As such, the term Pines-to-Palms Highway will be used throughout this book, unless the opposite has been used in a quote.

Acknowledgments

Any type of research undertaking such as this can never be done alone, and this book is certainly no exception. There were many people who helped me during the on-again, off-again research into this topic. For the various archives that I've accessed, I'd like to thank Jim Hofer of the Riverside County Archives, Randy Thompson of the National Archives in Perris, and Anthony Reed of the Frederick Law Olmsted National Historic Site in Brookline, Massachusetts. Similarly, Bob Smith of the Idyllwild Area Historical Society, Brett Romer of the Historical Society of Palm Desert, and Erica Ward of the Coachella Valley Museum were very helpful as always.

Harry Quinn, a Pinyon Flats resident for many years who has become the "go-to" person for information regarding the Coachella Valley and Santa Rosa Mountains, helped with the review of the manuscript plus with his recollections of what Arthur Nightingale told him years ago. Similarly, longtime friends and co-researchers Phil Brigandi and Nancy Wenzel reviewed the manuscript and offered several constructive comments.

Because Deep Canyon was mentioned several times in the contemporary accounts of the road for its scenic beauty, I wanted to go into it and get pictures for this work. Deep Canyon is a University of California research institute and is strictly off limits to the public. However, upon hearing of my research, Dr. Alan Muth, the institute's director, consented to my request and many thanks go to him for the experience. Thanks also go out to Mark Fisher, the Senior Museum Scientist, for taking the time to give me a tour of Deep Canyon.

Through the wonderful world

of the internet and sites such as Ancestry.com, I was able to track down descendents of many of the key players in the development of the highway. While they were surprised at my cold calls, they were generally grateful that someone was telling the story of their ancestors, and most were more than willing to allow me access to their personal pictures, for which I am very appreciative. These people include Lucille Cavanaugh (daugther of Charlie and Ophelia Tune, both of whom worked for Leo Honek), Marshal Cuffe (son of Frank Cuffe, one of the two federal sub-contractors), Sherwood Fulmor (grandson of Alexander Fulmor, the county's longtime surveyor), Dorothy Hayes (daughter-in-law of Barlett Hayes, Indio date grower and emcee at the opening ceremonies), Milton and Mellow Honek (son and grandson, respectively, of Leo Honek, the other federal sub-contractor), Steve Lovekin (great-grandson of Arthur Lovekin, an early proponent of a desert-to-mountain road), Eileen Maxfield and Harold Bump (grand-niece and grand-nephew of J. Win Wilson, Indio *Date Palm* editor and powerhouse behind the effort to build the Pines-to-Palms Highway), Gary McKenzie (grandson of Roderick McKenzie, the county's Road Superintendent), and Jim Wickerd (grandson of Elwood Wickerd, the superintendent of the county's prison road camp).

And lastly, I'd like to recognize J. Win Wilson and Wilson Howell. Of course, I never knew them, but their dogged tenacity, foresight, constant thought of community over self, and love of the region that draws me too brought about the Pines-to-Palms Highway as we know it today. Their ability to translate those qualities into something that convinced Riverside County residents and elected officials from the county, state, and federal governments, of the importance of the road to all of Southern California was truly remarkable. It is my hope that this book will instill some appreciation for what they did at a time when local projects like this were more appreciated.

Overall map of the Pines-to-Palms Highway showing route and contemporary place names.

Palms to Pines Highway, San Jacinto Mountains — Grey Photo

Chapter 1
Early Travel Between Mountain and Desert

    The Pines-to-Palms Highway is one of the most beautiful and awe-inspiring drives in Southern California. In the span of only 35 miles, a traveler can go from pine forests high in the mountains near Idyllwild and then travel through oak woodlands, pinyon-juniper woodlands, chaparral, and desert scrub brush, and end in the expansive Coachella Valley below. The highway opened in June 1932 amid great fanfare after a nearly 15-year effort to connect the San Jacinto Mountains to the desert below with a good high-gear automobile-accessible road. The story of the Pines-to-Palms Highway is a fascinating one, involving players who simultaneously wished for a good road for tourists and also for residents of the Coachella Valley.

    In order to understand how the Pines-to-Palms Highway was established, it is first necessary to delve into the history of travel in the area and the topography in which the road lies. In brief, the Pines-to-Palms Highway courses its way from Mountain Center to Palm Desert through a series of small, flat meadows and canyon edges that offer a distinct break between the San Jacinto Mountains to the north and the Santa Rosa Mountains to the south. Throughout its length, a traveler is continually shadowed by the aforementioned mountains on either side, until the desert portion of the highway is reached. In the cash-strapped 1930s, it is little wonder that the County of Riverside, the entity that built the majority of the road, was interested in saving money by running the road along lines that needed a minimum of grading and blasting to effect a level, smooth motorway. It is no accident, then, that the highway took the route that it did – however, there were many roads and trails in the area that it could have taken, and most of these roads had been in use for generations.

For thousands of years, the Cahuilla Indians lived throughout the San Gorgonio Pass, Coachella Valley, and San Jacinto/Santa Rosa Mountains area. As part of their subsistence patterns, they traveled between the mountains and desert as foodstuffs became available on a seasonal basis. Trails into and out of the mountains were vital to their ability to collect food and move between the higher and lower elevations as the seasons warranted. One of the earliest and most used trails led south from the village of *Sex-hi* (present day Palm Springs) up Palm Canyon to what is today Vandeventer Flats. Geographically speaking, the Vandeventer Flats area is at a crossroads of sorts. From here, not only did a trail lead down Palm Canyon, but there was a major trail that led from Vandeventer Flat east to Pinyon Flats, with smaller trails leading from Pinyon Flats down to the desert via Cactus Spring, Potrero Canyon, and Carrizo Canyon.[1] Likewise, additional trails led from Vandeventer Flats northwest into Garner Valley and the higher elevations, and west towards today's Anza Valley. These trails gave the early Indian inhabitants the ability to travel over the mountains in a relatively quick manner as opposed to circumnavigating them by going through the San Gorgonio Pass.

Pinyon Flats and the areas surrounding it were vitally important due to the huge stands of Pinyon Pines that produced Pinyon nuts, one of the staples of the Cahuilla diet. Another staple of their diet was acorns, which could be found in abundance throughout elevations higher than those at Pinyon Flats. By taking the trails from Vandeventer Flats northwest, the higher elevations were attained, as were areas for residing during the hot summer months. Therefore, the trails that ran between the San Jacinto and Santa Rosa Mountains and the desert below were vital to the Cahuilla's existence.

By the 1880s and 1890s, many of the aforementioned areas were being inhabited by white settlers who were coming to Southern California in droves. Throughout the San Jacinto Mountains and the Coachella and Cahuilla (Anza) Valleys below, many of these settlers were establishing cattle operations. Due to the nature of raising cattle, during the course of a year, herds of cattle would have to be moved between higher and lower elevations based upon the seasonal availability of water and food supplies. The new settlers soon discovered the old Indian trails and pressed them into service during cattle drives. It was not long before places such as the Hemet Valley (today's Garner Valley) and Vandeventer Flats saw herds of cattle being driven back and forth through the area. By this time, one of the old Indian landmarks in the area, a rancheria called *Gabelon*,[2] located at a spring at the foot of Santa Rosa Mountain, had been abandoned. Here, some of the cattlemen using the area erected a brush corral at the spring, which is very near the current entrance to the Spring Crest subdivision. This point became known as Brush Corral, and was used during the many cattle roundups and drives from the valleys into the mountains and back.[3]

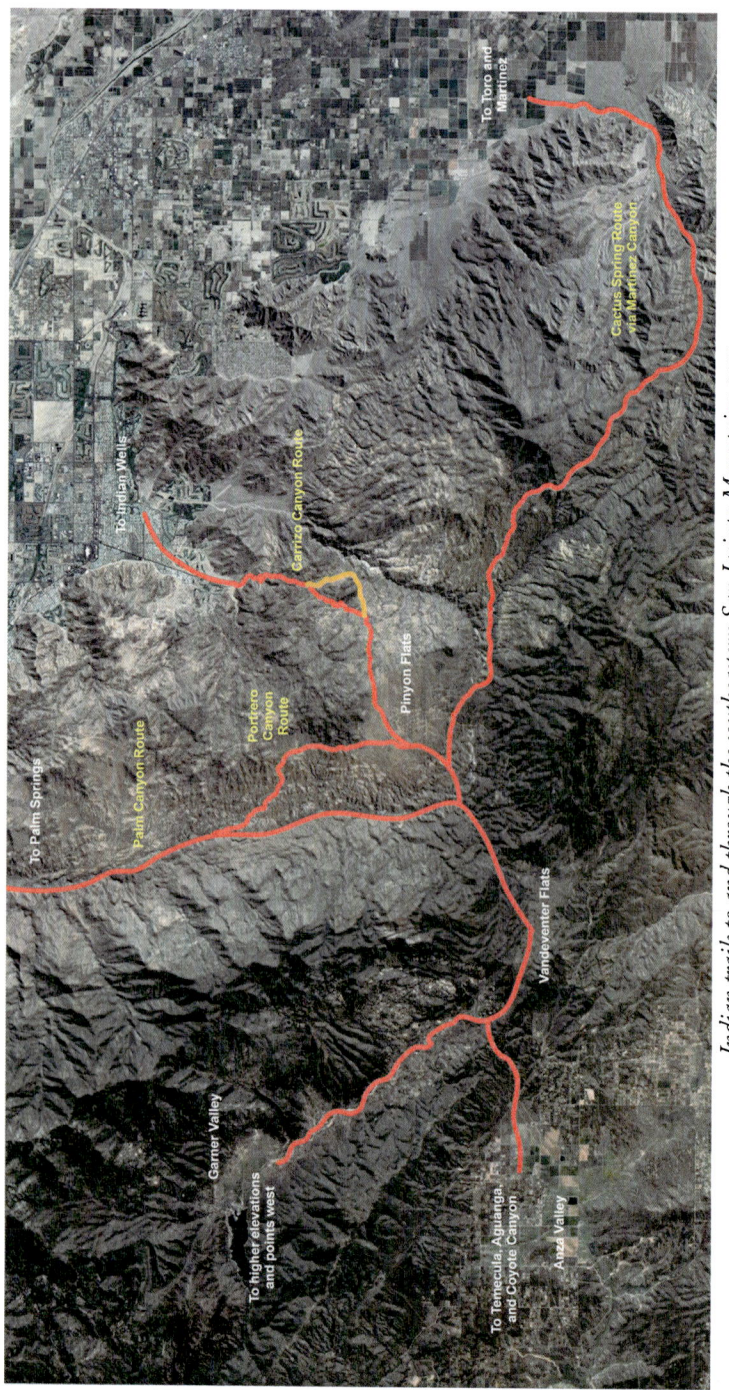

Indian trails to and through the southeastern San Jacinto Mountains area

These early Indian trails, though, and the many more that surrounded the San Jacinto Mountains to the north, west, and south, were not being used exclusively by cattlemen in these early years. Starting in the 1870s, residents and travelers from throughout Southern California seeking respite from the heat of the summer were discovering relief in the higher elevations. Travel from the town of Florida,[4] on the western slopes of the San Jacinto Mountains, up a winding road to Strawberry Valley, provided the beginnings of tourism in the area and the small town of Idyllwild that would eventually grow up with it. During this time, though, few of these tourists ventured along the Indian paths heading into the desert. That began to change around the turn of the 20th century, and it is at this time that we begin to see use of the term "Pines-to-Palms."

In April, 1905, Blanche Trask, a naturalist who wrote and lectured extensively about flora and fauna throughout Southern California, wrote an essay for the Los Angeles *Times* entitled "From Pine to Palm - Treasures of the San Jacinto Mountains." This seems to be the first time that the term Pines-to-Palms, or some variation of it, is used in print to refer to this section of the San Jacinto/Santa Rosa Mountains.[5]

At roughly the same time, George Wharton James, an ex-minister turned travel writer, journeyed through the area as part of his explorations of the San Jacinto Mountains and Colorado Desert. James, who traveled extensively throughout the Southwest and Southern California in the late 1800s and early 1900s, wrote about his adventures and the sites he saw. In his classic 1906 work *The Wonders of the Colorado Desert*, he devotes one whole chapter to a trip from the town of Florida east into the mountains, then down into the Coachella Valley. This chapter is entitled "From Pines-to-Palms," and describes his journey along the Hemet-Idyllwild Road to Keen Camp, thence southeast alongside Lake Hemet, then to the Garner Valley and Vandeventer Flats, where he enjoys the hospitality of both families. From Vandeventer's he takes Palm Canyon down into Palm Springs, and continues his journeys from there.

James is often credited with coining the Pines-to-Palms term in relationship to the San Jacinto Mountains area.[6] Although his book would have garnered much more publicity and for a much longer time than Trask's essay, it would be difficult to credit either of them with coining the term, since they were both touring and writing at the same time. Suffice it to say that by 1905, the term was in general use for the ability to go from the Alpine regions of the upper San Jacinto Mountains to the desert regions of the Coachella Valley relatively quickly (James' essay "From Pines-to-Palms" is included as Appendix B).

A third instance of the term in relationship to the region occurs in 1912. At that time, an unidentified writer for the Riverside *Press*, together with Dr. Robert L. Hill of Oakland and Morgan Draper, a civil and mining engineer from San Rafael, decided to blaze their own trail from Palm Springs to Idyllwild. Under the heading of "From Palm to Pine," they stated that, "our object was to find out whether a trail could be established which would connect the desert with the mountains, a trail from palm to pine."[7] Somehow, they determined that they were the first white men to attempt this.[8] Their trek led from the ridge between the west fork of Palm Canyon and Murray Canyon, went up the mountain toward what is now the ridgeline of Antsell Rock/Apache Peak/Spitler Peak, over to the ranch of Myron Onstott, then up to Keen Camp and Idyllwild, at which point they returned via roughly the same route. Although they were able to prove their point, nothing seems to have been done with this trail afterward.

Even though Hill, Draper, and the writer to the Riverside *Press* did not make a usable trail, one man in the area was inspired to do so. That man was Moses Sanborn Gordon,[9] a resident of Palm Springs with his own campsite/home in the mountains.[10] Gordon apparently wished to make a trail to connect the desert with the mountains above, and make it usable for not only himself but others. Starting in 1913, he spent four years constructing what he termed the "Pines and Palm Trail," working from the desert to the mountains during the winter months, and the opposite way during the summer. His trail started a little north of Andreas Canyon and headed up the precipitous side of Tahquitz Peak to the Tahquitz Valley and his campsite at Caramba.

Over the years, though, use of his "Pines and Palms" name waned, and it became known as the Gordon Trail, which is the name by which it is known today. Gordon's trail was opened in the summer of 1917 – "Always have we been told that a trail over this country was impossible, but this saying did not daunt Mr. Gordon, who worked it out during the past year . . . at an expense of about $1000."[11] Gordon was hailed as someone who had made a breakthrough that could be used relatively easily to get from desert to mountains – "M. S. Gordon of Palm Springs has constructed this trail 'from Pines to Palms' at his own expense . . . The trail is ten miles long and four years were consumed in its construction. Mr. Gordon has certainly made himself a public benefactor."[12]

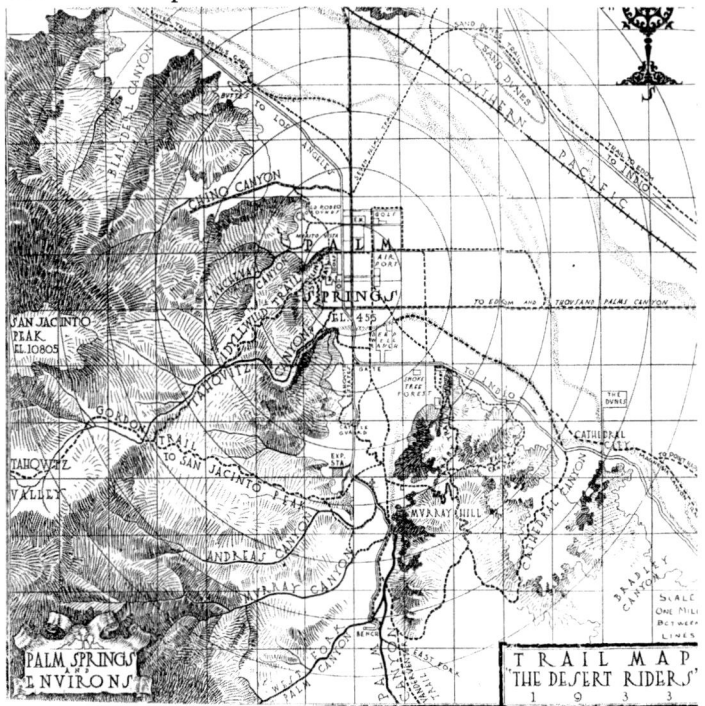

1933 Desert Riders trail map showing the Gordon Trail

A further instance of the term, coming into play just a few years before the Pines-to-Palms Highway in the San Jacinto Mountains, is the Jefferson Highway. The Jefferson Highway was planned in the mid 1910s to link New Orleans, Louisiana with Winnipeg, Canada. In its original configuration, it was to traverse the entire Louisiana Purchase, and was named as a memorial to Thomas Jefferson, who made the Louisiana Purchase possible. When launched in 1919, this highway was dubbed the "Pine to Palm Highway" colloquially because of its route from the forests of Canada to the shores of New Orleans. Soon, it took on two names, "Pine to Palm" for the trip south from Winnipeg, and "Palm to Pine" for the trip north from New Orleans. Although the highway was completed in 1926, the term "Jefferson Highway" soon lost out to regular highway numbering conventions. The route still exists today, but it is not generally referred to as the Jefferson Highway except by historians.[13]

Lastly, in the summer of 1925, in an attempt to garner support for preserving much of the San Jacinto Mountains, the Riverside County Chamber of Commerce asked Paul Shoup, the president of the Southern Pacific Railroad, to come to the mountains for the purpose of "visualizing the possibilities that exist for the development of a district that has one of the most remarkable views in the United States." In discussing the winter resorts of the desert and the possibilities for vacationing in the higher altitudes during the summer, they called for "a road from the palms to the pines . . . something that could not be secured in any other area of the country."[14] Clearly the thought behind this was to open up the mountain area to tourism, which is one of the main points that drove the creation of the Pines-to-Palms Highway.

Before the advent of the Pines-to-Palms Highway, residents of the Coachella Valley hoping to escape the heat of the desert by retreating to the San Jacinto Mountains had several options, all of which required a fair degree of fortitude and lots of time. No roads traversable by an automobile existed from the desert. Therefore, in order to get to the mountains quickly from the Coachella Valley, one had to either hike or ride a horse up one of the several trails available, such as through Palm Canyon, Dead Indian Canyon, or Carrizo Canyon. If one wanted to take an automobile to the mountains, a very circuitous route awaited. The driver had to leave the desert heading toward Banning and Beaumont. One option was to stop at Cabazon and ascend the mountain part way via the old Hall's Grade road which went as far as the present-day Lake Fulmor area.[15] If taking Hall's Grade was not to the driver's liking, before 1910, he would have to continue to Beaumont then head south into the San Jacinto Valley via either Lamb or Laborde Canyons. Once there, he would have to continue southeast to Hemet where he could pick up the old Hemet-Idyllwild Road and take that most of the way to Idyllwild. Near the head of Garner Valley the road split. Going north would lead to Idyllwild along a fairly well-maintained road. Turning south/southeast would lead down to Lake Hemet and Vandeventer Flats over

Hemet/Idyllwild Road, circa 1915

On the way to Strawberry Camp on the Hemet/Idyllwild Road, 1914

a fair road. After Vandeventer Flats was reached, the various roads out of that locale, mainly the old Indian trails mentioned beforehand, turned into rutted trails, and the motorist then had to be a hearty soul, because he did not know how or if he'd be able to go any farther.

Writing in 1960, Coachella Valley date grower and early Pinyon Flats homesteader Nina Paul Shumway described the journey from the desert to Pinyon Flats via Hemet taken before the modern highway came into being:

> . . . To reach the area by automobile was a roundabout all-day drive up through the Pass, over to Hemet, and up steep, narrow and crooked Idyllwild road on the far side of the San Jacintos. From there the route led through a long stretch of pasture land on the Garner Cattle Ranch, which necessitated opening and closing seven gates, followed by several miles of straddling Onstott Creek, climbing out of its rocky bed onto the old Asbestos mine road and dodging trees, brush, and granite outcrops across the Flat to the eastern slope which overlooked the Valley.[16]

In September, 1910, the first Banning-Idyllwild road was opened, which shortened the trip from the desert to the mountains considerably. This road started in Banning and continued south to the foot of the hills as it does today. Once there, it ascended the mountain via a road that had been constructed very roughly by Ed Poppet in 1885. Going through Poppet Flats, the road continued to Idyllwild in much the same manner that the present Banning-Idyllwild Highway does. This new road was a huge improvement for desert dwellers, but the fact still remained that if a desert resident wanted to get to the Pinyon Flats area (a distance of only about 10 air miles from the desert floor), there was still a trip of nearly 100 miles that had to be covered in order to get there. In addition to the inconvenience of the distance one had to travel to get to the mountains, there was also the fact that both the Hemet-Idyllwild and the Banning-Idyllwild roads were control roads. Due to several factors, many portions of both roads were very narrow. This necessitated the need for designating certain hours of the day for travel up the roads, and other hours for travel down the roads. If someone did not adhere to the prescribed schedule, or if someone was delayed for whatever reason, two cars meeting on the road would not be able to pass, thus making someone back down or up the hill to a place where it was safe to pass. The desire of desert residents to escape the heat of the region by going to the mountains, and the inconvenience of the two main existing motor routes to those mountains, began to concern leaders in Indio and other towns greatly, and thus the beginnings of what would become the Pines-to-Palms Highway.

Chapter 1 Notes

1. Contreras, Clarence, personal communication with Harry Quinn, as quoted in Quinn, 1997, pp. 35-36.

2. *Gabelon* was an Indian rancheria located at a spring right along present-day Highway 74 at the front of the Spring Crest subdivision, just east of the main entrance.

3. Contreras, Clarence, personal communication with Harry Quinn, as quoted in Quinn, 1997, pp. 35-36.

4. Florida was an 1880s boom-era town just east of Hemet. Today it is called Valle Vista, but the Florida name remains as the main thoroughfare (for more information on Florida, see Lech, 2004, pp. 458-460).

5. An extensive search for this essay proved fruitless. The only reference to it is an advertisement in the Los Angeles *Times* of April 15, 1905 indicating that the essay would be one of many special articles in the Sunday Los Angeles *Times* Illustrated Magazine for April 16, 1905. However, the Los Angeles *Times* Illustrated Magazine apparently was not kept during those years, and was certainly not microfilmed with the early editions of the regular newspaper. Queries to field biologists who know of Trask's work, along with several libraries, the Los Angeles *Times* archive, and the archive of the Automobile Association of Southern California were equally disappointing. It is still my hope, though, that some day a copy of this essay will be found.

6. See Gunther, 1984, p. 393 et al.

7. Anonymous. "From Palm to Pine." Riverside Daily *Press*, January 31, 1913. The full text of this trip is recounted in Appendix C.

8. Apparently they hadn't read James' book of six years before.

9. Moses Sanborn Gordon was born on December 14, 1854 in Exeter, New Hampshire and died September 27, 1940 in San Bernardino. In 1880, he was engaged in stock raising in Erath, Texas, living with the William Larner family. In 1900, he was listed as a widowed stock and ranchman, living with his two daughters Ruth and Esther in Weatherford, Texas. In 1910, he was a patient in the Loma Linda Sanitarium in the Mission District of San Bernardino. According to the 1920 census, he was living in the San Gorgonio Township (at that time, the region including Banning, Beaumont, Palm Springs, and all points in between), and had 2 borders. In 1930, he was back in the Loma Linda Sanitarium (Federal Census records and others, available on Ancestry.com).

10. This site was and still is called Caramba, or Camp Caramba.

11. "From Pines to Palms on the Gordon Trail." Riverside *Daily Press*, August 15, 1917. This description is reprinted as Appendix D, together with a later description by area resident George Law, who wrote of the "Pines and Palms Trail of Wonders" in the Los Angeles *Times*.

12. Gould, Louis Agassiz. "Hikers Take Fine Four-Day Outing." Los Angeles *Times*, September 9, 1917.

13. "Historic Jefferson Highway and the Links Between Winnipeg, Canada and New Orleans, Louisiana." http://maps.bc.ca/jeffhwy/index2.htm, accessed January 13, 2008.

14. Riverside *Enterprise*, June 22, 1925.

15. Hall's Grade, however, was not for the faint of heart. It had been carved out of the mountain in the 1870s by Col. Milton Sanders Hall when he received a contract to provide wood for the Southern Pacific Railroad. The road was quite steep, very treacherous, and was abandoned by Hall soon after its construction for a number of reasons, not the least of which was the fact that he had lost several horses and men to the steep road (for more information on Hall's Grade and Hall City, see Lech, 2004, pp. 250-252).

16. Shumway, 1960, p. 263. The "Flat" referred to is Pinyon Flats, and the "Valley" is the Coachella Valley.

Asbestos Mountain and Pinyon Flats

Chapter 2
Initial Proposals and Construction Efforts

While Morgan Draper and his cohorts, and Moses S. Gordon after them, were trying to find trails to take them from the desert to the mountains, others had loftier goals of constructing an automobile-accessible road for the same purpose. By 1919, proposals to create either a National Park or State Park around most if not all of the San Jacinto Mountains were making serious headway, and two Riverside County boosters believed having a road from the desert to the mountains was necessary.[1] In April of that year, Riverside County Supervisor Rowley Smith, together with Arthur Lovekin, a farmer and entrepreneur from Riverside,[2] announced a plan to have the County of Riverside construct the "Rincon Trail Road," an easy automobile road that would lead from Palm Springs up Palm Canyon to Vandeventer Flats, then, using existing roads through Garner Valley to Keen Camp, take motorists all the way to Idyllwild. This road would be called the Rincon Trail Road, since it would essentially pave and straighten the existing

Rincon Trail up Palm Canyon.³ The two men unabashedly described the proposed road, and the Riverside *Press* echoed their enthusiasm:

> This route was known as the Rincon trail, and it is still used by government forest rangers in their work. That this old trail can easily be made a superb mountain highway is certain, Mr. Lovekin states. And when Riverside county has completed this new road, which will be 12 miles in length, the widely advertised Rim-of-the-World drive in San Bernardino county will be equaled if not surpassed in scenic wonders.⁴
>
> The consummation of the plans evolved by Mr. Smith and Mr. Lovekin will mean that Riverside county will have within its borders an attraction which will spread the fame of this county and its beauties the length and breadth of the continent. . . . [O]ne of the best things about the whole idea is that the construction of the 12 miles of new road up Palm canyon should cost comparatively little. Considering the incalculable value to the county as an asset for bringing tourists here, as well as for the enjoyment of local vacationists, the cost will be negligible.⁵

Arthur Lovekin with his wife Helen with their children Osgood and Charlotte
(Photo courtesy Steve Lovekin)

The Hemet *News* was equally enthusiastic about the prospects of such a road:

> It would afford an ideal automobile trip, connecting the present road to Idyllwild with the Coachella Valley country, by way of the famous Palm canyon and springs. From Palm canyon to Vandeventer Flats there is a rise of 3,900 feet, and it is believed the road could be made to take this in easy grades.
>
> From Vandeventer Flats there are to be had wide vistas of dropping mountain, foothill and valley, views that fairly take one's breath away. Standing on the running board of his car the motor tourist or camper may gaze off toward the Warner's Ranch country, in San Diego County, toward the broad Pacific.[6]

Needless to say, Lovekin and Smith's enthusiasm was shared by many who could see the tourism benefits of such a road, along with the practical ones. Opening the San Jacinto Mountains to the desert and vice versa could have untold benefits from tourism. The Riverside County Board of Supervisors agreed with Lovekin and Smith, and on April 28, 1919, instructed County Surveyor Alexander Fulmor to complete a study of the proposed route, which would include his recommendations as to the road's feasibility and cost of construction.[7] Fulmor, however, was occupied with several other county-sponsored road projects during this time. It was not until September, 1920, that he and Kenneth Dickerson, the county's Superintendent of Road Construction, journeyed to Palm Canyon to begin their work.[8]

On March 9, 1921, Fulmor submitted to the Board of Supervisors a report indicating not only a possible route, but that that route was feasible to construct.[9] Under Fulmor's proposal, the road would start at Keen Camp, taking off

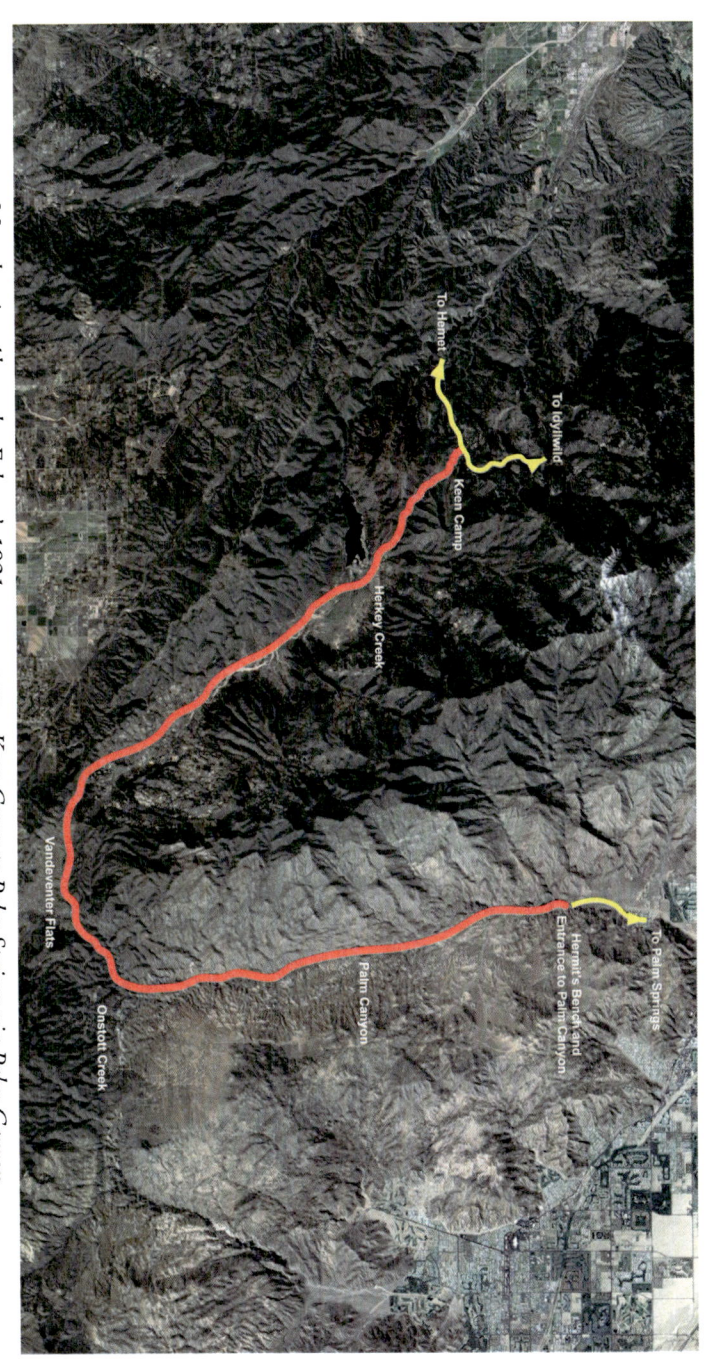

Map showing Alexander Fulmor's 1921 survey route - Keen Camp to Palm Springs via Palm Canyon

A. C. Fulmor

Alexander Fulmor
(Photo courtesy Riverside County Survey Department)

from the existing Hemet-Idyllwild Road. The new road would then lead down to Vandeventer Flats along the same route that had been open for years. Fulmor indicated that since this stretch of the road had already existed and was in good shape, the entire 18-mile stretch could be brought to standards for approximately $4,500. From that point, though, the real construction would begin.

The next four miles would go from Vandeventer Flats northeast, along the west slope of Palm Canyon. Fulmor considered this to be "rough, rocky country," and estimated that it would cost $7,500 per mile to complete that section. From there, at a point near the confluence of Palm Canyon and Onstott Creek,[10] the road would follow the bottom of Palm Canyon for 13 miles, all the way to the connection with the existing road from Palm Springs to Palm Canyon, at approximately where the Hermit's Bench lay.[11] All told, the entire stretch, according to Fulmor, would be 35 miles in length from Keen Camp to Palm Springs, and cost approximately $80,000 to construct[12] (the full text of Fulmor's report is included in Appendix E).

William Pester - The Hermit of Palm Springs

30

Vandeventer Flats

The 1921 survey by Fulmor did show a practical route, but the county lacked the resources necessary to build it at that time. While there was great enthusiasm for the road, the Rincon Trail Road was not the only one being considered in Riverside County. Throughout the early 1920s, Riverside County engaged in several road-building endeavors. These new roads were completed for two basic reasons - for the benefit of the citizens of Riverside County of course, and for the benefit of the many tourists who were visiting the area during the winter months. It must be remembered that from as early as the 1870s, people began coming to the region to escape the effects of winters in the mid-west and east coast. In addition, in the days prior to the mass onslaught of automobiles and superhighways, most people were content to spend their vacations nearby, either in one of the many hot springs resorts, the mountains, or the desert. Therefore, as a way of fostering tourism in the 1910s and 1920s, when automobile travel was becoming very popular, the Board of Supervisors embarked on many road building projects throughout the county.

This was helped along by statewide efforts in the form of bonds to raise money for road building. Beginning as early as 1909, and continuing through the 1920s, several bond measures were passed statewide for road construction. For example, July 2, 1921 saw the approval of $40 million in State bonds specifically for road construction. With that in mind, many roads were proposed to be constructed or improved throughout the county and state. In Riverside County, some of these included the Jackrabbit Trail (the main route between the San Jacinto Valley and the San Gorgonio Pass), a badly-needed Palm Springs to Indio Highway, a revamping and upgrade to the Banning-to-Idyllwild road, and another that would connect Banning to Palm Springs via Whitewater.[13] These roads and several others were given higher priority, because they would be used by more people. Therefore, backers of a mountain to desert route would have to wait a few more years.

Early photo of the Banning-Idyllwild Road

The next time the idea of the mountain-to-desert road was given any serious consideration was during December 1925, when Alex Fulmor escorted a group of Los Angeles area newspapermen along much of the proposed trail that he had surveyed more than four years previous. His reason for leading this trek was to garner support for the proposed road. Several of the roads mentioned above had been constructed, and there appeared to be an opportunity of put forth the proposal for the mountain-to-desert road again. From a publicity standpoint, his trip was very successful, and Willard S. Wood of the Los Angeles *Times* concluded that,

From [Vandeventer Flats] to Palm Springs, Riverside county hopes to build a connecting road. Seventeen miles of new road down Palm Canyon and a small sum spent in widening and grading the road from Keen Camp to Vandeventer Flat would complete a loop road unexcelled in interest in all Southern California. "Approximately $80,000 would open such a road to travel," Fulmor told us as we stood at the summit of Palm Canyon and looked out over the Colorado desert. "The grades would be easy and the road presents no difficulties whatever from an engineering standpoint."

If such a road were built it would be unique among all the highways of the United States. The present road to Palm Springs down the San Gorgonio Pass is wonderful, with its unforgettable view of the sheer 10,000 foot wall of San Jacinto from the north. Through Palm Springs and into Palm Canyon the road would lead, with the hosts of native palms growing beside the canyon pools. On through the palms and cottonwoods of Little Paradise the road would climb by easy stages to the 5000 foot summit at the head of Hemet valley, and the pines and rushing mountain streams of San Jacinto canyon.[14] The contrast from palms to pines, and from the warmth of sheltered desert canyons to the sharp airs, and snows of winter on San Jacinto would make the round trip over such a road an experience unequaled in all the calendar of American motoring.[15]

Fulmor's desire for the mountain-to-desert road came at the same time that residents and civic leaders in western Riverside County could see that the most traveled route up to Idyllwild was the one through Hemet. That road, though, was old, hazardous, and in desperate need of being upgraded if it was to continue to entice automobile-bound tourists to the region. Starting in the early 1920s, proposals were put forth to improve the road from Keen Camp to Idyllwild, and also greatly upgrade and reconfigure the Hemet-Idyllwild road into a good, high-gear road that would be a showcase avenue for Riverside County. By early 1926, serious consideration was being given to this idea, and on March 8, 1926, the Board of Supervisors resolved to begin improving the road while trying to obtain help from the federal government for the effort.[16]

The delay in improving the Hemet-Idyllwild road had more to do with economics and the necessities of other portions of the county than anything else. Improving and building roads is expensive, but by the mid-1920s, another avenue to road building was open to the Board of Supervisors. In 1925, Sheriff Clem Sweeters began advocating for the establishment of a county prison road camp that would house inmates whose sole job was to construct, improve, and maintain county roads. The physical work of performing the wanted improvements would be made much easier and less expensive to Riverside County at a time when such camps were becoming the norm throughout the State of California. In November, 1925, the Board agreed with Sweeters and established such camps by resolution.[17] The first of these camps in Riverside County was located near Gilman Hot Springs in San Jacinto, the labor being used for the construction of Foothill Boulevard (today's Gilman Hot Springs Road). When that was completed in March 1926, and the Board of Supervisors was approving work to begin on the road to Idyllwild, Sheriff Sweeters asked that the camp be moved "to near Keen Camp."[18] The move was made, and the inmates in the prison camp began work on the Keen Camp–Idyllwild Road while the Board sought an agreement with the federal government for the much larger Hemet-Idyllwild road. That agreement was reached in March, 1927, and for the next few years, construction on a new, realigned, and automobile-accessible road between Hemet and Idyllwild was performed by both the federal government and prison labor under the auspices of Riverside County.

In April of 1926, at the same time a new Hemet-Idyllwild road was being put into the limelight, leaders from throughout the Coachella Valley came together to discuss the conditions of roads in the area in general, and what improvements should be made. Within an area dubbed the Indio Permanent Road Division, discussions centered around paving the highway between Palm Springs and Indian Wells and improving a road that would lead from Indio to the San Bernardino County line through Fargo Canyon (to better access the mining areas of the desert). However, the greatest proposal came from an idea to merge the Hemet-Idyllwild road with one to the desert:

> The new road between Hemet and Idyllwild [would] be extended through Keen Camp and to Vandeventer Flat, thence down Palm Canyon to intersect the Indio-Palm Springs road. . . . So far as we have been able to sound out public opinion on the west side of the mountains, everyone says our proposition is a liberal one and should be taken up by the board of supervisors without debate.[19]

The proposed mountain-to-desert road would be the exact same as the one proposed five years earlier. This time, though, the road would be advertised as going clear from Hemet to the Coachella Valley, which would make a shorter route for all concerned. As proposed, the three-road project in the desert was to be spread out over three years and cost around $175,000 to complete.[20]

The proposal for a mountain-to-desert road was different this time, in that there were two strong backers who had the wherewithal to garner support for the proposal. The first was John Winfield (J. Win) Wilson, the influential editor of the *Date Palm* newspaper of Indio. Wilson was born in Sac County, Iowa on December 25, 1869 and came to Indio in 1909, spending his first few years there as a farmer. On March 12, 1912, he began the *Date Palm* newspaper which put him

John Winfield (J. Win) Wilson, Editor of the Indio Date Palm
(*Photo courtesy Marshall Cuffe*)

on the road to becoming a very influential leader in Indio. By the 1920s, his connections through both business and personal interests were such that he could get most things done that he put his mind to.[21]

Wilson's partner in this case was another Wilson - Wilson Howell Jr. Howell, the son of Wilson Howell of Thomas Edison's Menlo Park laboratory, had come to Indio around 1919 after a stint as an aircraft inspector during World War I. He farmed 2½ acres in Indio, and began one of the first mail-order fruit businesses when he started shipping his ripened grapefruit all over the country. Often, Howell would escape the heat of the desert by climbing the Dead Indian Canyon trail to the foot of Santa Rosa Mountain. Howell was not as wealthy or influential as J. Win Wilson, but Howell knew people, knew the lay of the land, and had some experience in surveying, which would prove to be an asset.

36

J. Win Wilson was determined to get a mountain-to-desert road, so in April, 1926, he began the process of appealing to the Board of Supervisors by submitting petitions to them outlining his desires. At various meetings held in Indio in early April, he circulated the petitions, and submitted them to the Board at their regular meeting of April 26. At that meeting, Wilson explained that a mountain-to-desert road as that proposed would "not only furnish another means of access to the San Jacinto mountain district, but would ultimately give a thorough route for tourists crossing the projected Ehrenberg bridge near Blythe from Indio to Riverside via Hemet."[22] The supervisors filed the petition but withheld a decision at that time.

This action by the Board gave Wilson further opportunities to gather support. To do this, Wilson and others took their idea west, and pitched the mountain-to-desert road to their counterparts in Hemet. There, they indicated that the proposed road would make for a shorter trek to the desert, and it would bring a large amount of traffic from the Imperial Valley and points farther east into the Hemet area. Business and civic leaders in Hemet and the surrounding areas agreed, and offered their support for a mountain-to-desert road.[23] Petitions were signed, and Wilson continued his campaign in not only the desert and Hemet areas, but also the San Gorgonio Pass area too.

On June 7, 1926, the Riverside County Board of Supervisors took up the matter of the proposed

Wilson Howell at Ribbonwood along the Pines-to-Palms Highway

desert roads, and listened to the arguments put forth by Wilson and several others from the desert and Hemet areas. J. Win Wilson, ever the salesman, had even received a letter of support from King Gillette, the safety razor manufacturer.[24] After hearing Wilson's case, the Board agreed with all of his points, but could do little about it at the time. The Hemet *News* reported that the Supervisors indicated:

> . . . that there are no county funds available at this time for so large an undertaking, but they would be willing to go as far as their finances would permit. . . . [I]t is practically impossible to make the roads a major project this year as funds would not be available to cover the cost . . . Supervisor Hancock, in expressing the attitude of the board as being favorable to such improvements from the standpoint of opening up new territory and adding to the value of mountain and desert property, outlined the demands which already confront the board in the making of the next budget.[25]

In the end, the Supervisors denied the petition to begin work on the mountain-to-desert. They did, however, give tacit approval for it, only to be built later. They agreed to fund a survey for the road, but made it clear that the new Hemet-Idyllwild road, which was already approved and funded, would be built first. The spirits of the mountain-to-desert road boosters were lifted, however, when the supervisors announced that the Hemet-Idyllwild road would be the "first link in the chain which will eventually reach from the desert through the mountains and to the county seat."[26]

Although his proposed road was postponed for now, J. Win Wilson lost no time continuing the push for his dream. On June 18, 1926, he published a forceful editorial in the Indio *Date Palm* where he told readers the virtues of developing the mountain areas of Riverside County. The editorial below sums up the overall reasons very succinctly;

Our grand old mountains, that have stood undisturbed through all the ages, are to be tamed and made into a playground for all of Riverside county; yes, for all the world. This much was made clear when the road boosters went before the supervisors a week ago last Monday. There is no doubt about it; the whole county is back of the movement.

And there are no grander mountains anywhere on earth than right here in Riverside county. Outside of building roads that will develop the farms and the mines, our next best bet is roads that will develop the mountains.

Next to food for the body, man needs food for the soul. And where can one get a better meal for the soul than in the mountains, where God has always held close communion with man.

Aside from the well being of the citizens of Riverside county, the development of the mountains also means the well being of the county treasury. Those rocks and crags, and pines and brooks, can be made to yield shekels of the realm, even as the desert has been made to yield onions and dates.

In these days of transportation and commercial intercourse, one's property is valuable in exact proportion to the number of people that pass one's door. This is true of the mountains, as it is true of Seventh and Broadway. If ten thousand cars a day pass up Palm canyon and out of the mountains by way of one of the western routes, that portion of the mountains will pay taxes to Riverside county in exactly the same proportion that property on Seventh and Broadway pays taxes to Los Angeles county.

The 1926 delay in constructing the mountain to desert road also gave Wilson time to think. By the next year, his attention had shifted away from a road to the mountains via

Palm Canyon and toward a more southerly route that would bring access to the higher elevations closer to Indio. He had heard of an old Indian trail that led from the desert up to Pinyon Flats. In May and June, 1927, he and a few others tried several times to find it. On June 10 they did:

> After once finding the starting place, the trail was well defined and easily followed. That it has been in use for thousands of years is plainly evident. In some places where the rocks are of a soft character, it is worn down to as much as 12 to 18 inches deep.
>
> The first half mile of the ascent was pretty steep and we soon added a thousand feet to our elevation. The rest of the way up the grades are easy and uniform and the hikers made good progress. By half past twelve we were on the east slope of Black mountain and the country was open and rolling. We estimated that we had traveled in our winding course about 4½ miles and were a little over three miles from where we left the automobile. . . .The important point that we determined is that a road is quite feasible. There is about half or three quarters of a mile of rather stiff construction. The rest of the route is largely a matter of rolling boulders to the low side of the road. With the proper equipment . . . we estimated that a passable single track road could be built for $6,000 or $7,000. Three thousand dollars more would make a good single track road, and $25,000 would make a boulevard. . . . It should be bourne in mind that this road would give the Coachella valley every advantage that a road up Palm Canyon would by connecting up with Idyllwild and the other resorts on the west and south slopes of the mountains. And that it has the advantage of being much cheaper and shorter.[27]

Only a week later, Wilson was boldly calling this prospective route a "proposed road," and by mid July he and

Carrizo Canyon (top) and Dead Indian Canyon today

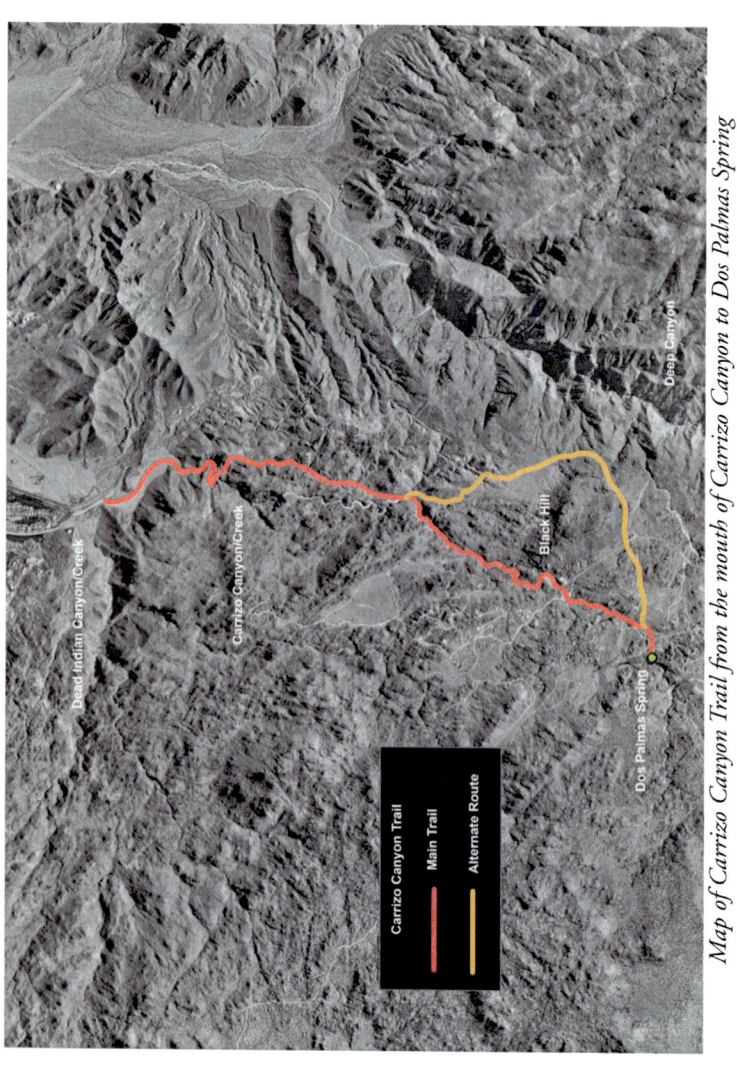

Map of Carrizo Canyon Trail from the mouth of Carrizo Canyon to Dos Palmas Spring

some unnamed cohorts had already placed signs along this newly-discovered (to him) route to help his fellow Coachella Valley residents find their way along the shorter route to Pinyon Flats.[28] Wilson was convinced that this southerly route, in essence along the Carrizo Creek trail, would be a much better route to the mountains and would be much closer to his adopted town of Indio. Therefore, over the next few weeks, Wilson discussed the virtues of Carrizo Creek and Canyon and Dead Indian Creek, Canyon, and Falls in the pages of the *Date Palm*, all of which were scenic places at the base of the mountains and along the new route. In doing this, he hoped to get as many residents of the Coachella Valley to discover the route and see for themselves how much easier it would be for them to ascend to the higher elevations closer to home.

Throughout the summer of 1927, J. Win Wilson continued his campaign for what he was now calling the Dead Indian Trail.[29] On August 6, he sponsored a picnic at Dead Indian Canyon together with Indio date grower Dana G. Sniff, John W. Newman of Thermal, and Austin B. Martin, a concrete pipe contractor in Indio.[30] Obviously Wilson had been busy in the background, for on the morning of August 7, he and his picnickers awoke to the arrival of Stephen A. Nash-Boulden, the U.S. Forest Service's supervisor for the Cleveland National Forest. For the next few hours, Wilson, his party of residents, and Nash-Boulden hiked up the Carrizo Canyon Trail, alongside the eastern slope of Black Mountain, then over to Dos Palmas Spring, where the

> . . . easy grade brought us out on top of the universe. We could look away down into Deep Canyon and away off across Horse Thief creek to Santa Rosa peak, that is more than 8,000 feet high. A mile to the west we could see the pine trees of Pinon Flats peeping over the ridge to us, and we were assured by the foresters that there is no road problem to be encountered from that point on.[31]

Looking into Deep Canyon from Cahuilla Tewanet

Nash-Boulden was very impressed with the prospects of Wilson's proposed road and promised the full cooperation of the U.S. Forest Service in the endeavor. Building the first mile or two would be the toughest, they determined, but it would not be insurmountable.[32]

Wilson's efforts now turned to making *this* road a reality. The 4-5 mile stretch that would make the connection between the desert and the mountains would be the toughest, and therefore should be at the forefront of his efforts. Since the prospects of Riverside County building the road soon were remote, Wilson turned to the formation of a special district that would levy taxes upon those parcels within the district to fund construction. Wilson proposed to form a district encompassing just over 2.5 million acres of mostly desert land under the California State Boulevard District Law which allows for property owners to petition for establishment of such a district. With an assessed valuation of nearly $3.25 million, the district could, it was reasoned, easily put together the roughly $25,000 - $30,000 needed for construction of the road. Wilson and others circulated petitions for signatures, and on December 2, 1927, formally petitioned the Board of Supervisors for such a district, backed by petitions signed by

93 property owners mostly in the Indio area. The supervisors responded by setting a hearing date of January 3, 1928 to fix the boundaries and to set up an election.[33]

On January 3, the Board removed sizable portions of the proposed district due to protests from large land owners and the Southern Pacific Railroad's land company. Despite arguments from Austing Martin and J. Win Wilson, most of the Chuckwalla Valley area was similarly excluded. After this reduction of area, the Board indicated that it would fix a date for a hearing at the next meeting, due to be held on January 9.[34] There was a sizeable amount of support for this project:

> There is no project more worthy of support than one which will make the cool mountain areas more accessible to the people of the desert country in the hot summer periods. As it is at present, it is a long, hard drive to reach the summit of mountains that are looking down upon the valley from its western side and it seems unfair that the residents of the desert should practically have to encircle the mountains to get to their cool valleys and resort possibilities.
>
> There are many thousands of acres of possible cabin sites and resorts that may be opened up if an adequate road is erected to San Jacinto. It is a project that has been favored for some time in the possible form of a continuation of the road now being built by prison labor at Keen Camp, which it is suggested will reach Palm Springs within the next two or three years.[35]

On January 9, though, Wilson and his supporters were given bad news – the Board denied their petition for formation of a boulevard district. Upon review of the law by District Attorney Albert Ford, it was found that the provisions of the boulevard district required the sponsoring county to contribute 25% of the cost of construction and maintenance to the district.[36] Wilson and his supporters were not in attendance, so word of the denial was written to them. This made them angry, and Wilson showed up to the next meeting asking the reasons behind the refusal. Stating that the Board had no discretion in setting the boundaries and election, Wilson's attitude outraged Supervisor Thomas Flaherty, who accused Wilson and his supporters of bad-faith because they didn't inform the Board of the 25% contribution requirement.[37] Despite the animosity, the Supervisors asked the District Attorney to recommend some form of a compromise. After making the delegation from Indio wait until all of the Board's business was completed late in the day, the Board proposed that instead of building the road under the auspices of the Boulevard District, perhaps it could be done under a road improvement district. With a proposed cost of $35,000, the county's share under this plan would be only $5,100. Plus, they would promise to have the survey work done on the proposed route starting immediately upon the submission of a petition to form road improvement district. This proposal was acceptable to Wilson and the other delegates. Therefore, they were to go back to Indio, circulate new petitions under a road improvement district, and come back to the Board at an early date to enact this new compromise.

On February 6, 1928, the group was back in Riverside before the Board, this time with petitions signed by over 160 residents asking for the formation of a road improvement district to construct the Pinyon Flats-to-desert road. They found the Board "more amicable" this time, and the Board took immediate action upon their request. They ordered County Surveyor Alexander Fulmor to begin a survey of the proposed route as soon as practicable and to give them an initial report by February 20.

The survey and report took until March 10 (the full text of Fulmor's survey can be found in Appendix F). At that time, Fulmor indicated that the road could be built, built easily, and would be of great benefit not only to the residents of the Coachella Valley but also the county as a whole. However, the

5-mile portion described by Wilson and his supporters would only get people to a point about 4 miles from Pinyon Flats. Although a rough road existed between Vandeventer Flats and Pinyon Flats, it was certainly not up to standards for tourists. Therefore, when he did his survey, Fulmor took into account putting a road all the way through to Vandeventer Flats. The problem with his proposition, though, was that the total cost for all construction, in his estimation, was $76,500 – fully 2½ times the amount believed necessary and achievable by Wilson and his cohorts.[38] At this time, it was becoming more and more apparent that this road would need to be a county-sponsored road and not simply a local road as proposed by Wilson and the others:

> What the promoters had in mind was to "gum out" a single track road that could be used until the county prison camp and other resources could be brought into action and the road widened and improved to the extent that the traffic demands.
> It is quite true that the road is to be a thru county road and all the county is to benefit by its construction. This fact is beginning to penetrate the minds of the west end of the county and it will continue to grow. The road will be built. It is only a question of having it done as soon as possible and at a cost that we can afford.[39]

With the release of Fulmor's survey and recommendations, posturing for a road from Keen Camp to the Coachella Valley began immediately. At the Board of Supervisors meeting on March 12, 1928, several representatives from the Chambers of Commerce of both Palm Springs and Banning appeared before the Board to ask that the prison camp be retained in the San Jacinto Mountains and that a survey be commenced immediately for a road from Keen Camp to Palm Springs to be routed down Palm Canyon.[40] The Board took no action, and this seems to have quieted down the rancor for the road for the next year.

Meanwhile, with the notion that the County Surveyor believed that the Dead Indian Canyon route was the best and most feasible, and the fact that there was only a 4-mile "tough spot" between the desert floor and the higher country, J. Win Wilson and Wilson Howell began to take matters into their own hands. Stating that "County Surveyor Fulmor has layed out a much better grade up the mountain than any of us had hoped for, and it is going to cost more money, so there will be nothing for the valley portion of the road for some time. . . . We all want to use the present road this summer and will want to use it for some time. Therefore, it is considered good policy to make a bee of it and put the road into shape for use."[41] Wilson and Howell organized what constitutes a work party on March 4 to drag the road between the end of the pavement on the Palm Springs-Indio highway and head south into Dead Indian Canyon. What Wilson called a "bee"[42] turned out to be a big success and the road work was done that afternoon. Similarly, on April 1, the two put together a party to go over the route from the mountains. Inviting people from the desert and the Hemet/San Jacinto area, this group Was to meet in Hemet, go up to Keen Camp, then take the existing roads down to Pinyon Flats via automobile. Once at the end, they would hike down the Carrizo Canyon trail to the mouth of Dead Indian Canyon where more cars would be waiting to take them back. "The idea is to give everyone a chance to see for themselves whether the proposed Pinon Pines road is really worth while. . . County Surveyor Fulmor will be in the party and will walk down over the proposed road with any one who wishes to make the trip."[43]

Throughout the summer and fall of 1928, Wilson Howell took several people along the route in the high country via automobiles to show them the merits of the route. He found three additional springs in the Pinyon Flats area that were much touted as additional necessities for both people and automobiles. Similarly, articles appeared touting the virtues

Wilson and Howell's rough road to Dead Indian Canyon, 1928 (present-day intersection of Highway 111 and SR 74 looking south) (Photo courtesy National Archives and Records Administration)

of the lower temperatures in the canyons and the need to make them easily accessible from the desert.[44] Several articles appeared which indicated support for the Pinyon Flats route from Riverside, Oceanside, and other places throughout Southern California. If nothing else, J. Win Wilson kept the proposed route in the limelight.

Despite the arguments and appeals for a road leading from the mountains to the desert, actual construction would not begin until October, 1929 - fully one year later. The County of Riverside was still engaged in constructing the Hemet-Idyllwild Road, surveying a road from Elsinore to San Juan Capistrano (which would eventually become the Ortega Highway), starting work on constructing an addition to the Riverside County Courthouse, and paving the roads from Hemet to the Oak Cliff Ranger Station and Palm Springs to Indio.[45] Another road such as J. Win Wilson wanted so desperately would have to wait. The issue, of course, would not die – and the next year was used in posturing between two main factions in the desert. One that wanted a road from Keen Camp to Palm Springs via Palm Canyon, and the other led by Wilson that wanted the road routed via Pinyon Flats. This contest would last nearly two years and be the object of intense lobbying on both sides.

Chapter 2 Notes

1. The efforts to create some form of officially-sanctioned park in the San Jacinto Mountains would be varied and take many different directions. Although these efforts happen at the same time as the efforts to create the Pines-to-Palms Highway, a lengthy discussion of the development of a park is beyond the scope of this work. If the reader is interested in knowing more about the development of San Jacinto State Park, please see Davis, 1973.

2. Little could be determined about Rowley Smith. He was born in Kansas on August 22, 1873. He was young when he came to California, for when he was 6 he was living with his parents in the Wilmington area of Los Angeles. By 1900, he had married his wife Lottie and they were living in Santa Ana where he was a salesman for a farm implement company. He spent the four years from January, 1919 to January 1923 as a Supervisor from the 5th District. In 1917 he described himself as a rancher living in San Jacinto, whereas both the 1910 and 1920 census list him as a farmer from Hemet. By 1930, he is selling real estate in San Jacinto. At the time of his death in Long Beach on March 14, 1954, little information could be gleaned about him for an obituary (Fitch, 1993, p. 14, Federal Censuses for 1880, 1900, 1910, 1920, and 1930, California Death Index 1940-1997).

   Arthur Lovekin was one of many early Riverside County residents who performed a great deal of civic duties, but about whom little is known. Prior to his coming to Riverside in 1905, he had been a banker and a farmer in his native Canada. He came to California in the 1880s, and worked as a surveyor in Los Angeles, and then as a gold miner in Shasta County. When he arrived in Riverside, he purchased land on Olivewood Avenue, built a house, and planted several acres of orange groves. He became very influential in the area, and also worked to develop a great deal in Blythe and the Palo Verde Valley. There, he is honored by having Lovekin Boulevard named for him.

   More germane to the story here, though, is that Lovekin was one of the leaders who campaigned to establish Mt. San Jacinto State Park. He served on several committees for that establishment, so it is little wonder that he would have become intimately involved in the effort to establish a mountain-to-desert highway.

   In 1936, Lovekin had to return to Canada for health purposes. When he left, he donated his property in Riverside to the Riverside City College, which named his home Lovekin Hall. The present Lovekin Complex on the RCC Campus continues that tradition (Riverside *Daily Press*, June 22, 1949).

3. Rincon Trail received its name from the Indian village of Rincon. According to George Wharton James, Rincon was located near the mouth of Andreas Canyon:

> About midway between Palm Springs and Palm Canyon a dim wagon-road turns off to the right which leads to the mouth of Andreas Canyon. Just before entering it, however...the deserted Indian village of Rincon may be seen, in a small, narrow valley. It is close to the foothills. Here for many years the Indians had their unpretentious habitations. They brought water down in little ditches from Andreas Canyon and planted figs and grapes and sought in their simple fashion to improve their condition. Dr. Murray aided them in procuring seeds and they seemed to be progressing, when a wealthy white man of Riverside, with a selfish disregard for their rights, 'took up' the water of Andreas Canyon, piped it down to his 'Garden of Eden' and left the Indians waterless (1906, pp. 292-293).

Dr. Murray is Welwood Murray, well-known early resident of Palm Springs and Banning, and keeper of a sanitarium at Palm Springs for many years. The "Garden of Eden" was a development scheme by Burleigh B. Barney of Riverside during the boom times of the 1880s. It was located northeast of Andreas Canyon. Like so many development schemes of that era, it failed and left a mark for years. George Wharton James did not mince words when discussing the Garden of Eden and its impacts on the local Indians:

> When I inform my readers that this was done for purely speculative purposes, as practically next to nothing has been done to improve the Garden of Eden, the strong language used to designate the contemptible conduct of some white men toward the Indians will not be deemed too severe. The Indian agent of that day was not inclined to put himself out to defend the rights of his people and they were soon "dried out" and compelled to move elsewhere (1906, pp. 292-293).

For more on the Garden of Eden, see Lech, 2004, pp. 286-288.

4. The Rim-of-the-World Drive is a 101-mile long drive in the San Bernardino Mountains that connects San Bernardino and Redlands to the mountain communities of Lake Arrowhead, Crestline, Running Springs, and Big Bear. It opened July 18, 1915 and quickly became a huge success and a tourism bonanza for the area (http://www.rimoftheworldhistory.com/region.html, accessed December 4, 2011).

5. Riverside Daily *Press*, April 10, 1919. Curiously enough, on April 25, 1919, the Hemet *News* ran an article entitled "Rincon Trail Road Again Contemplated." This seems to indicate that at some time before, the issue was brought forth, and that the present (1919) proposal was simply a resubmittal of the original. However, a check of the Riverside Daily Press from 1910 to 1919, and the Hemet *News*, the *Date Palm* of Indio, and the Riverside County Board of Supervisors' Minutes from 1915 to 1919 failed to bring to light any previous discussions or attempts.

6. Hemet *News*, April 25, 1919.

7. Riverside Daily *Press*, May 1, 1919.

8. Riverside Daily *Press*, September 8, 1920.

9. Riverside County Board of Supervisor Minutes, March 9, 1921.

10. Onstott Creek (also called Omstott Creek) was named for one of the many mountain characters of the time, Myron M. Onstott. A native of Illinois, Onstott came to the Guapa area west of Riverside, settled there for a while, then later moved up to the Santa Rosa Mountain area. There, he lived a hermit's life, befriending many campers and travelers in the area. When he died in February 1908, the Los Angeles *Times* wrote of him:

> As a result of exposure to the bleak winds and snow of the San Jacinto Mountains, M. M. Onstott, who is known to perhaps every camper in this part of the State, died at his lonely mountain cabin. Word was received yesterday of the passing of the old man, who had lived the life of a hermit as far back as the memory of his oldest friends goes.
>
> A few days ago a party of hunters from the valley went on a camping trip to the mountains and stopped at the Onstott cabin. There they found the old man prostrate on the floor and almost dead from cold and lack of the remedies needed in his illness. The visitors started a fire and did everything possible to revive him. Then one of their number returned down the mountain grade to San Jacinto for a physician. Pneumonia set in and although the doctor made a swift race with death, he arrived too late.
>
> Onstott lived on a secluded ranch two miles north of Keen Camp. He had a thorough education, was a most interesting conversationalist, and was liked by everyone who knew him.

Why he chose to live alone in the solitude of the mountains was always a mystery to his many friends. (Los Angeles *Times*, February 13, 1908; Gunther, 1984, pp. 362-363).

11. Hermit's Bench (referred to also as Hermit's Haven) was the name given to the overlook above Palm Canyon. It was named for William Pester, an individual who immigrated from Germany in 1906 and went to the desert to live a hermit's existence. Presently, the Hermit's Bench is the location of the gift shop in Palm Canyon. An interesting article about the Hermit's Bench/Haven appeared in the Los Angeles *Times* in 1917:

> Hermit Haven is Next to Nature
>
> Palm Canyon is interesting spot for the tourists to visit.
>
> Hermits who voluntarily relinquish their share in the benefits and comforts of civilization, are wise men when they select a climate like that of Southern California in which to pursue their solitary way.
>
> One spot, over in Riverside County, seems particularly designed by nature to harbor such recluses from society. The air is perennially soft and warm. Even at night - a sparkling pool of clear water is almost surrounded by clumps of palms - and the circling hills form a natural barrier against wind and storms.
>
> This "Hermit Haven" (not so well known as it deserves to be) is Palm Canyon, reached by auto through Beaumont, Banning and Palm Springs - and the palms that give it its name are the only California "Native Sons" in the palm family. These along grow naturally in Southern California, all the other palm trees found here have been brought in from somewhere else.
>
> The hermit in question is one of the unique characters of a region abounding in queer types. He went to live in picturesque Palm Canyon a good many years ago, when his broken health demanded an out-door life.
>
> Anyone who sees him now will need no other testimony as to the physical benefits of life in this favored vale. He finds the air so warm and the sunshine so pleasant that he has almost entirely discarded clothing and his diet is also on a "near to nature" basis. . . . Fruits, nuts and vegetables furnish his food, and a more active and physically striking example of the virtues of vegetarianism is rarely seen.

Although the visitor in its quiet depths might imagine himself hundreds of miles away from civilization, as a matter of fact, Palm Canyon is quite accessible over a plainly marked, well made road, the route being fully described in the "Book of Southern California Tours" issued by the Goodrich Touring Bureau. The only part of the trip which does not provide good automobile roads is the three miles from Palm Springs into the canyon. This stretch is very rough, but a party of eastern visitors who recently covered the ground . . . found it easily negotiable. They were certain that the unique and interesting features of Palm Canyon scenery are well worth the journey. The return to Los Angeles can be made over the Jack Rabbit Trail from Beaumont to Riverside, one of the finest mountain highways both in construction and view to be found in America. (Los Angeles *Times*, December 2, 1917)

12. Fulmor, Alexander. Report to the Riverside County Board of Supervisors, February 17, 1921, as reprinted in the Indio *Date Palm*, April 30, 1926.

13. The *Date Palm*, Hemet *News*, Riverside *Daily Press*, various dates.

14. Little Paradise is a place approximately half way up Palm Canyon. It was a little oasis in the canyon, with cottonwoods in addition to the ubiquitous palms. Hemet Valley refers to the area that contains Lake Hemet. It is unknown what Wood is calling San Jacinto Canyon - it could be either Garner Valley or South Fork Canyon where the present Highway 74 leads from Hemet to Mountain Center.

15. Wood, Willard S. "Mountain Pass Crossed Century and Half Ago." Los Angeles *Times*, December 27, 1925.

16. Riverside County Board of Supervisors' minutes, March 8, 1926.

17. BE IT RESOLVED and proclaimed by the Board of Supervisors of Riverside County that an Industrial Road Camp has been established in the said County of Riverside and this 23rd day of November, 1925 is hereby designated the day on and after which persons will be admitted to such Camp who have been sentenced to imprisonment in the Industrial Road Camp for violation of Sections 270 or 270 (a) of the Penal Code, or of misdemeanors in the Superior Court or any Justice Court with the County.

Upon motion of Supervisor Johnson, seconded by Supervisor Hancock and duly carried it is ordered that the following resolution be adopted as follows to-wit:

BE IT RESOLVED that a Superintendent of the Industrial Road Camp be employed at a salary of $150.00 per month and board and lodging at said Industrial Camp, and

BE IT FURTHER RESOLVED that it is necessary for the proper administration of said camp and the keeping of the prisoners therein to employ for each ten prisoners one guard and the compensation of each guard is hereby fixed at $90.00 per month and board and lodging at said camp, and

BE IT FURTHER RESOLVED that every person imprisoned at said road camp be credited with a sum of $.35 per day for each day of eight (8) hours work done by him at such camp, and that such persons who shall be in the manner provided by law, to have any person or persons dependent upon him for support shall be credited with such additional sums as may be fixed by law. (Riverside County Board of Supervisors Minutes, November 23, 1925).

18. At the location near Keen Camp, the county leased approximately 12 acres of property from William and Viola Johnson just north of the Hemet-Idyllwild road. On March 2, 1931, the Board authorized the purchase of the property from the Johnsons for $800, and a permanent prison road camp was established, allowing the temporary camp to be moved to the Aguanga area.

19. The *Date Palm*, April 30, 1926.

20. The *Date Palm*, April 30, 1926.

21. Los Angeles *Times*, December 24, 1930; United States Federal Census, Indio Township, 1900 and 1910.

    John Winfield (J. Win) Wilson was born December 25, 1869 in Wall Lake, Sac County, Iowa to John W. and Annie Wilson. He grew up in Iowa, but when he was 28, he accompanied his parents and siblings to Oregon where they settled mainly in the Monmouth area.

J. Win Wilson then went to Duluth, Minnesota for a while, working as a chemist for the U. S. Steel Corporation. However, the cold got to him so in October, 1909, he came west to the Coachella Valley and settled on a farm in Indio. There, he farmed for a few years until March 12, 1912 when he set aside his farming implements and started the Indio *Date Palm*, one of Indio's two newspapers for several years (the other being the Indio *News*). His first wife, Hannah, died in 1914, and in December of the next year he married a widow from El Centro named Josephine Eddy.

Wilson became a stalwart supporter of many improvement projects throughout the Coachella Valley, and had the vehicle to express his opinions. Throughout the rest of his life, he worked for many years to get the Palm Springs-Indio Highway constructed, and then helped to develop U. S. Highway 99 through Indio and beyond so that residents and tourists alike would pass through the town. He was instrumental in laying out the route to Blythe that the present-day I-10 follows. He was on the Board of Fire Commissioners for Indio from its inception in 1924 until 1937. Knowing that Indio

John Winfield and Josephine Wilson
(Photo courtesy Marshall Cuffe)

needed large hotels to attract and keep visitors, he helped to form the Indio Sanitation District to sell bonds and create a sewer system so that larger hotels could be built. In the late 1920s, he also helped to form the Indio Levee District which constructed earthen berms to divert flood waters around the town, thereby protecting life and property.

Above all, he was known as a person who held nothing back when it came to promoting Indio and the Coachella Valley. If someone got in his way, Wilson fought back. He accomplished much in his nearly 30 years living in Indio, but still wanted to do more when, on the evening of June 29, 1937, his wife Josephine found him slumped over in his chair, the victim of a massive stroke. He was rushed to the Coachella Hospital where he died Sunday, July 4, at the age of 67, having never regained consciousness. His old rival newspaper, the Indio *News*, said of him, "Aggressive and unafraid, Mr. Wilson played no favorites in his campaign for the advancement of Coachella Valley. Those in high places many times felt the sting of the virile editor's justified criticism. Ignoring flowery phrases, Mr. Wilson wrote frankly and bluntly when he felt there was a wrong to be righted." Wiley Magruder, who took over the *Date Palm* from Wilson in his later years, said "I do not believe there is another man in Coachella Valley today who has expended as much energy in behalf of the community as J. Win. Wilson put forth in his twenty-seven years here. No other man has accomplished as much for the community, certainly."

22. Hemet *News*, April 30, 1926, Riverside *Press*, April 26, 1926.

Another of the many road building projects to occur in Riverside County at this time was the construction of a toll bridge across the Colorado River that would connect Blythe to Ehrenberg, Arizona. This bridge was ultimately built by a private company, the California-Arizona Bridge Company, and was opened in March 1928 (California Highway Commission, 1929, pp. 43, 101, 102).

23. Hemet *News*, May 7, 1926.

24. Hemet *News*, June 11, 1926.

Gillette was a major landowner in the Palm Springs area, and was apparently rather well known to some of the town's residents.

25. *Ibid.*

26. *Ibid.*

The Riverside *Press* (May 7, 1926) also commented on the road, stating that,

> there is a well organized movement not only for a better highway in the mountains from Hemet and San Jacinto, but also a road from the Coachella valley by way of Palm canyon. That improvement may not be realized for some time, but it is entirely feasible and should be worked out as soon as county funds permit. When that

Mt. San Jacinto from Garner Valley

road is built, it will be possible to drive from the Hemet-San Jacinto valley over the mountain range and down into the Coachella valley through the wonderful Palm canyon. That trip could be one of the most remarkable and spectacular in the country. The improvement of the highway from this side of the mountain should however be given first consideration; and the county can only do a limited amount of work of this character in a year.

Mount San Jacinto is one of the great assets of the county and the development of its possibilities has only begun. The attractions are there - unique, abundant and varied; but their proper use is dependent on good roads. That is the urgent problem that the county faces; and the Press commends the supervisors and their purpose to work out a program to meet it.

27. Indio *Date Palm*, June 17, 1927.
28. Indio *Date Palm*, June 24 and July 15, 1927.
29. Wilson referred to this as Dead Indian Canyon trail, although it is and was generally referred to as Carrizo Canyon Trail. Dead Indian Creek empties out onto the alluvial fan in a broad swath and, of the several creeks in the vicinity, is the major one. Ebbens' Creek and Carrizo Creek come out of the hills just to the south and feed into Dead Indian Creek as it heads north toward the lower elevations. However, the actual trail that Wilson and his party took led further

south from the mouth of Dead Indian Canyon (which runs toward the west). At the entrance to Carrizo Canyon, the trail leads along the sandy bottom then goes up onto the ridge and back into the canyon a few times to avoid some very tall waterfalls.

30. Indio *Date Palm*, August 5, 1927.
31. Indio *Date Palm*, August 12, 1927.
32. Indio *Date Palm*, August 5 and 12, 1927. The first mile or two would be what is today the Seven Level Hill.
33. Indio *Date Palm*, December 16, 1927.
34. Indio *Date Palm*, January 6, 1928.
35. Riverside *Enterprise*, January 24, 1928.
36. Indio *Date Palm*, January 13, 1928.
37. Indio *Date Palm*, January 20, 1928. Wilson could not help himself recounting the conversation in the pages of the *Date Palm* –

    "Flaherty to Wilson – 'Did you know that this 25 percent provision was in the law?'

    Wilson – 'Certainly I did.'

    Flaherty – 'Then why did you not tell us so?'

    Wilson – 'Why didn't you ask me? You were telling me all the time what YOU knew.'"

38. Indio *Date Palm*, June 22, 1928.
39. Indio *Date Palm*, March 16, 1928.
40. Indio *Date Palm*, March 16, 1928. This is the beginning of the 2+ year battle over which route the Keen Camp to the Desert road would take. This battle is the subject of Chapter 3 and will be covered in depth there.
41. Indio *Date Palm*, March 2, 1928.
42. A "bee" in this sense is like a communal work party, not unlike a quilting bee.
43. Indio *Date Palm*, March 30, 1928.
44.   CANYONS ARE COOLER BY ACTUAL TEST
    (Indio *Date Palm*, May 18, 1928)

    Last Sunday promised to be a warm day and a desirable one for a trip to some of the nearby canyons. Now in making a quick selection of some place to go, one should always remember that the Dead Indian canyon is the most desirable for two reasons. There is water and there is elevation with the least possible distance and the best road.

So the the old Scout Car was trundled out and headed for the west on the Palm Springs road. The party was joined by Wilson Howell and Miss Josephine Carter, in an other Ford, and the new road drag, provided for by Mrs. C. D. Clarke was loaded on as a part of the equipment.

Arrangement was made with Walter Richie at the Indio Drug Store No. 2 to read the thermometer every hour and keep a record. The start was made at 11:00 a.m. the temperature standing at 100 degrees.

Mr. Schisler, the new real estate man, went along as far as the old Ray Merritt ranch, where a little time was spent and a little business for the old Indio Levee District was attended to. When we arrived at the turning-off place on the highway and started up the Dead Indian road, the Scout Car took the drag in tow and Wilson Howell followed behind to throw out the rocks that it loosened up.

By 1:00 p. m. we had proceeded up the mesa 3½ miles and the thermometer in the car registered 101½. At Indio the thermometer stood at 107.

By 2:30 p. m. we had arrived at the shade of the canyon and removed the thermometer from the car. It was standing at 102. But on being hung on a mesquite bow it soon dropped to 94. At Indio the thermometer in the shade of the drug store was standing at 108. Here was a clear difference of 14 degrees.

By 3.00 p. m. the Indio thermometer had dropped to 107 and ours had dropped to 93. Still a difference of 14 degrees. By 4.00 p. m. our thermometer had dropped to 92 but the Indio thermometer was still standing at 107. Showing a difference of 15 degrees. At 5.00 p. m. the Indio temperature was registered at 98 while in the canyon it was shown to be 88.

There is a difference of about 1,200 feet in the altitude of the two places, and a clear difference of not less than one degree of temperature per 100 feet of altitude. The distance from Indio is exactly 16½ miles. The thermometers were later compared by hanging them beside one another, and found to register exactly the same - 83 degrees.

(Cont.)

The Why of the Pinon Pines Road

If these rates should continue to hold good as we ascend the mountains, and there is no reason to expect anything different, 2,500 feet of altitude would give us a difference of 25 degrees. We can get it in less than 20 miles from Indio.

An elevation of 3,500 feet should give us a lower temperature of 35 degrees. We can get it with water at Dos Palms Springs in 22 miles from Indio. The Van Deventer Flats with an altitude of 4,500 feet and lots of live oak shade, should give us a 46 degree lower temperature. We can get it in 29½ miles from Indio. That is the why of the Pinon Pines road.

45. Riverside County Board of Supervisors' Minutes, various dates. The addition to the County Courthouse was done by G. Stanley Wilson and completed in 1931 on the rear of the existing building. This is the side that fronts Orange Street. Paving the two additional roads was quite necessary to access the new Oak Cliff-Idyllwild Road and to make a paved highway all the way to Indio.

The Coachella Valley from Vista Point along the Pines-to-Palms Highway

Chapter 3
Controversy Over The Route

The Pines-to-Palms Highway was built foremost as an economic route to bring tourists to and through the lower Coachella Valley and San Jacinto Mountains. In a time when towns were eager to attract tourists and passers-by, it was only natural that several factions would develop to advocate not only for the building of the road but also for a route that would be most beneficial to their own interests. The Pines-to-Palms highway was no different. As was shown in the previous chapter, the decision to build the road had been made – what wasn't clear was just how the road would get to the desert from the mountains. Well before construction commenced in October, 1929, people from throughout the Coachella Valley, western Riverside County, and Southern California in general began to align themselves with groups that touted one of many ways to route the proposed road. For nearly 24 months, the route that the new road would ultimately take was a matter of controversy, argument, meetings, editorials, petitions and multi-day tours to show decision makers the benefits of one route over the other. Before construction began, the factions geared up for a fight – one that brought impassioned pleas and charges of favoritism on the part of many.

The paramount question was how a road could be built from the mountains to a connection in the desert that was relatively inexpensive, opened up the greatest amount of land for use, and offered the greatest number of people easy access to the mountains. Most people were in agreement that the section from Keen Camp to Vandeventer Flats was the best way for the beginning of the road to lead from the mountains to the desert (although by no means the only). However, how it would get from Vandeventer Flats to the desert was where the controversy really began. Eventually, three routes came to the forefront of this controversy – the Palm Canyon Route, the Pinyon Flats/Dead Indian Canyon Route, and the West Fork of Palm Canyon Route.

Palm Canyon looking south

The Palm Canyon Route

This route was the basis of planning for a mountain-to-desert road beginning with Arthur Lovekin and Rowley Smith's proposal in the 1910s. Since Palm Canyon terminates at Vandeventer Flats, this proposed route would lead from Vandeventer Flats and head northeast along the west side of Palm Canyon and then continue north for approximately 15 miles, criss-crossing Palm Canyon a few times to take advantage of better terrain for laying a road. Ultimately, the road would come to the Hermit's Bench at the mouth of Palm Canyon, where an existing improved road would take travelers directly into Palm Springs.[1] This route had the advantage of aligning itself with a world-renowned tourist destination (Palm Canyon), and of being the closer of the routes to the larger centers of population from which to draw visitors, namely Riverside and Los Angeles. Naturally, this route was championed by business and resort owners in Palm Springs.

The Pinyon Flats/Dead Indian Canyon Route

This route was the one devised by J. Win Wilson and Wilson Howell and came about as a desire by residents of the lower Coachella Valley to have a closer connection to the mountains and relief of the summer heat. This route would lead due east from Vandeventer Flats to Pinyon Flats. From Pinyon Flats it could either travel along the south edge of Pinyon Flats, around the south side of Sugarloaf Mountain, then head northeast along Deep Canyon to Black Hill, or it could go northeast through Pinyon Flats to Asbestos Spring, then east to Dos Palmas Spring and then to Black Hill.[2] Either way, both routes would then travel north along the east face of Black Hill, descending into the desert via a modified version of the centuries-old Carrizo Creek trail.[3] Here the road would head north, cross Dead Indian Creek at the mouth of Dead Indian Canyon, and then continue northeast to a connection

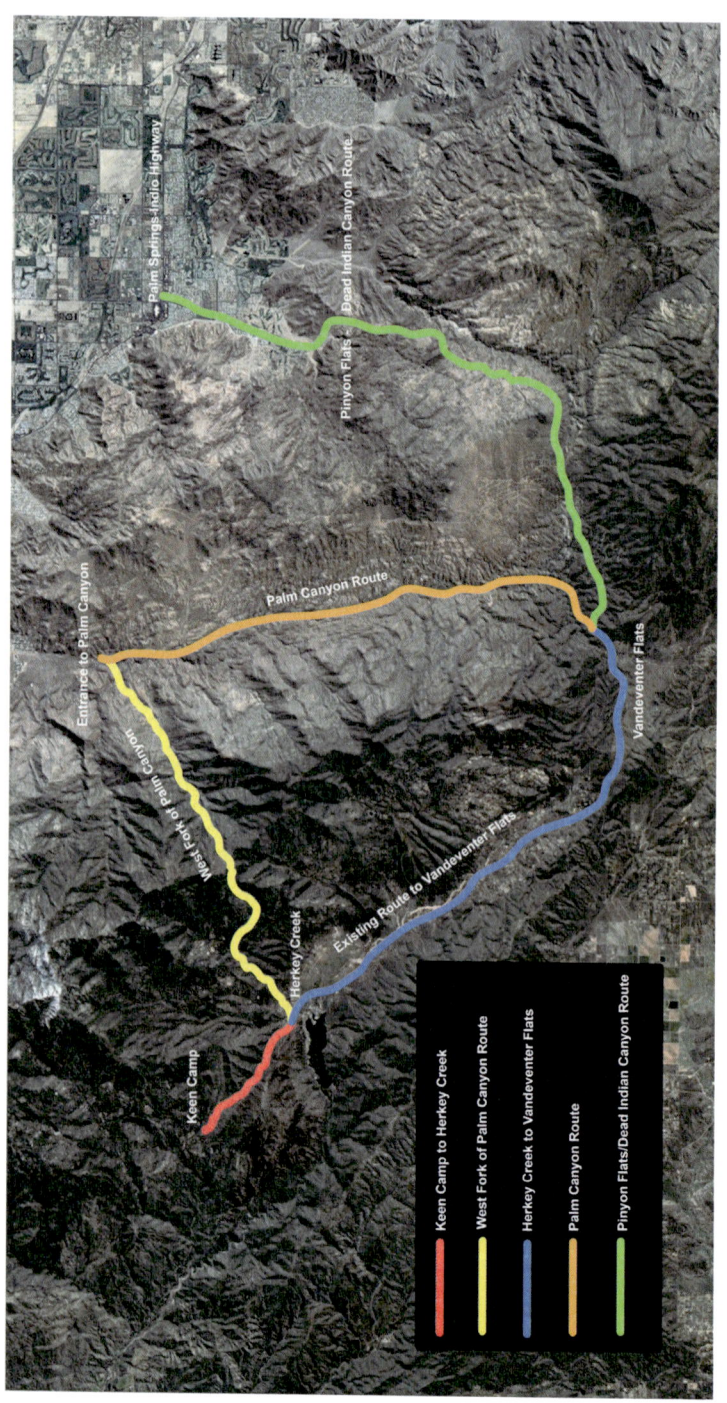

Map of the possible routes for the Pines-to-Palms Highway

Inside Carrizo Canyon

on the Palm Springs-Indio Highway approximately 12 miles west of Indio. This route had the advantage of being closer to the desert communities of Indio, Coachella, and Thermal, along with being a shorter route for people entering the San Jacinto Mountains from the Palo Verde and Imperial Valleys. This route was heavily championed by factions in Indio, along with many of the aforementioned communities.

The West Fork of Palm Canyon Route

This proposal was put forth by yet another entity working to promote the San Jacinto Mountains. In March, 1929, the San Jacinto Mountain State Park Association, which, understandably, was much more interested in public access to the proposed park than opening up land for development purposes, proposed a much shorter route to the Idyllwild National Forest Highway. Their proposal still left from the connection at Keen Camp, and still continued southeast for a few miles, but then took an abrupt turn to the east at Herkey Creek[4] and would continue due east toward what is today called Spitler and Apache Peaks,[5] although those peaks were unnamed in the 1930s.[6] The road probably would have ascended the

Spitler and Apache Peaks

ridge between Spitler and Apache Peaks, using a series of switchbacks due to the very steep terrain.[7] Once over the ridgeline, the route would have descended along the West Fork of Palm Canyon, leading to the base of Palm Canyon and then to Palm Springs. This route would have been a nearly straight-line route from the desert to the Keen Camp area, but would have gone through some very rocky and precipitous country to achieve the shorter route. This route had few supporters beyond the San Jacinto Mountain State Park Association.

The opening salvo in the controversy came on March 12, 1928, when several representatives from the Chambers of Commerce of both Palm Springs and Banning appeared before the Board of Supervisors. Their objective was twofold – keep the prison camp in the San Jacinto Mountains so that the much cheaper prison labor could be retained for road building in that area, and ask that a survey be commenced immediately for a road from Keen Camp to Palm Springs to be routed down Palm Canyon.[8] This request was a direct result of the positioning of J. Win Wilson relative to having the county build a road from the same place but through Pinyon Flats to Dead Indian Canyon as outlined in the previous chapter.

West Fork of Palm Canyon, 1929
(Wieslander Vegetation Type Mapping Collection, courtesy of the Marian Koshland Bioscience and Natural Resources Library, University of California, Berkeley, www.lib.berkeley.edu/BIOS/vtm).

The various factions were told unequivocally that no more road building would take place in the San Jacinto Mountains until the Hemet-Idyllwild road was completed, and that the completion of the road was at least a year away.

Supporters of the mountain-to-desert road took note and reappeared almost exactly a year later. On March 11, 1929, Palm Springs Chamber of Commerce Secretary and bank manager Phillip Boyd, together with several other leading individuals from Palm Springs, Riverside, and Banning, appeared before the Riverside County Board of Supervisors to ask them to conduct another preliminary survey of a road from Keen Camp to Palm Springs via Palm Canyon. Boyd and his cohorts stated that the Board should undertake this project, especially since prison labor was available in the San Jacinto Mountains.[9] Plus, it was reasoned, work on the Hemet-Idyllwild Road was nearing completion, and that offered a perfect opportunity to begin work on the next phase, namely the mountain-to-desert road. Dr. Ernest Clarke of Riverside, who was the Riverside County Chamber of Commerce President, joined Boyd in offering the Chamber's endorsement of the road. However, the Chamber did not recommend that the road go through Palm Canyon, only that any decision on the route should be left to the Supervisors to choose the one most practicable. All were in agreement, though, that the road should be built to State standards so that the State could eventually take over maintenance of the road. Supervisor Harvey Johnson, summarizing the Board's meeting in the Banning *Record*, indicated that "the new road, wherever built, should be of such a standard that it could be taken over by the state at any time. Success of the San Jacinto Mountain park will, of course, bring state funds for roads within the park. The building of a road of standardized specifications would undoubtedly bring federal aid." Once again, the Board took no action at that time.[10]

Apparently, the Board members had a change of heart, especially given that popular support for a mountain-to-desert road was growing. Just two weeks later, on March 25, the Board ordered Riverside County Surveyor Alexander Fulmor to conduct a preliminary survey of a road from Keen Camp to the desert side of the mountain. They specifically mentioned the "desert side of the mountain" instead of Palm Canyon or Pinyon Flats to leave open the possibility of multiple routes. The point here was to have Fulmor investigate not only the physical routes but also the possibilities offered by all three proposed routes together with their respective advantages and disadvantages.[11] Fulmor stated that he would begin the tentative work within a month, and would examine at least three possible routes.[12] Upon hearing that the Board had authorized this survey, the ever-enthusiastic J. Win Wilson stated that:

> Any of the possible routes from Keen Camp to the desert will be at least 30 miles in length, and will go through territory now practically untouched by roads or trails.
>
> Besides furnishing a magnificent scenic route, such a road would provide an adequate means of penetrating unprotected forest and brush lands in a large area, should forest fires occur.

View of Palm Springs' downtown, circa 1930

View of Indio's downtown, circa 1927

Choice of the route will depend considerably upon the territory which would be opened up, as well as from the standpoint of providing a new scenic route which would complete the circuit about the San Jacinto mountains.[13]

Just a week after the Board session wherein Fulmor was instructed to begin a survey, Phillip Boyd reappeared to invite the Board on a tour over the Palm Canyon route. The Board of Supervisors accepted, and discussed plans for not only a tour of the Palm Canyon route but also the Pinyon Flats route.[14] This would allow all supervisors to familiarize themselves with the routes and also have an opportunity for the various factions involved to make a show for their respective routes. The tour began on Monday, April 15, 1929 when the Board members and approximately 20 others, including state park and road officials, newspaper reporters, chamber of commerce officials, Emanual T. Mische (a renowned park designer and protégé of John Charles Olmstead), and even a representative of Frederick Law Olmstead, met at the Idyllwild Inn for the night.[15] The next day, they drove to Vandeventer Flats where a group of horses awaited them from Palm Springs. The rest of the day was spent traversing Palm Canyon to Palm Springs where they had a formal dinner before spending the night at the Desert Inn. The next day, they set out for the mouth of Dead Indian Canyon, where J. Win Wilson had prepared a large group of people to meet them in anticipation of their trip up the Carrizo Canyon Trail and on through Pinyon Flats. This tour took all morning, and by Wednesday evening the groups were back in their respective towns to contemplate what they had seen over the past few days (Riverside *Press* reporter Jessica Bird's detailed account of the journey is reproduced as Appendix G).

The tour was a success and the Board members, together with the many other individuals who had an interest in the road, all felt it worthwhile to explore the two main route proposals.

A decision, though, on which route would eventually be chosen was contingent upon Alexander Fulmor and his crews who were just beginning their work of surveying. One source was quoted as saying it would take approximately six months to complete the survey and calculations for both the costs and the amount of dirt and rock that had to be moved. Due to the importance of the road to Riverside County and Southern California as a whole and the intensity of the arguments that were being made for and against the various routes, Fulmor wanted to be very sure that he covered all of the territory affected by the routes, and that his final recommendation could not be called into question due to bias or mistaking some important element along the way.

Therefore, for the next six months, little was done to decide which route the road would eventually take. This interim time was used mainly by J. Win Wilson and the other Pinyon Flats route supporters to tout the virtues of that route, how much the road was needed and would aid in the area's economy, and how many other groups/persons/towns joined with them on their side. In an editorial entitled "Palm Groves vs. Palm Gardens," Wilson stated:

> Considerable has been said of late about building a million dollar road up Palm canyon to show off the wonderful palm groves there. It is said that they are a great asset to the county and will attract many tourists there. All of which sounds good until we reflect that there are dozens of other canyons with palm groves in them that are much more accessible than Palm canyon.
>
> But the question that is uppermost in our mind is: What's the matter with showing off the date gardens and grapefruit orchards of the Coachella valley? Here we have something that is wonderful and cannot be matched anywhere else in the world. More than that – they have an economic value.

Survey crew, 1920s. Alex Fulmor stands far right, and partner James Davidson stands far left (Photo courtesy Sherwood Fulmor)

They produce something good to eat. They give employment to the wage earner and revenue to the taxpayer with which to keep the county government going. They are good for something more than to look upon. And there are many other things in the Coachella valley that are unique and great attractions to Riverside County.

If we are to build mountain roads that rank among the most expensive in the world for the purpose of showing off some of our attractions, why not show off something that is worth while? ...

Our date and grapefruit growers are largely dependent upon the tourist trade for the marketing of their products. The cash customer that stops at the roadside stand and buys the farmer's produce is the best customer he has. It would not cost Palm Springs people anything to permit cash customers to make contact with the Coachella valley farmers, and it would do us a lot of good.

It will not cost the people of Palms Springs anything to support the Pinon Pines road and thereby benefit the farmers of the Coachella valley greatly.[16]

Throughout the spring and summer of 1929, surveys of the proposed routes continued while work on the Hemet-Idyllwild Road began to wane. On May 28, 1929, the new Hemet-Idyllwild road was officially opened, although a few months of follow-up work would still need to be done. All of the parties involved hoped to have the new road open for the summer season, and the work crews obliged. With work on the Hemet-Idyllwild road winding down, it was hoped that the Board would authorize the beginning of the road to the desert. That announcement came on August 16, when the Hemet *News* stated that the Board of Supervisors had authorized work on the mountain-to-desert road to begin within 60 days, with work on the Hemet–Idyllwild road to finish within 30 days (the beginning of construction of the Pines-to-Palms Highway will be covered in Chapter 4). With this announcement, fervor over the proposed routes escalated. As the onset of construction on the desert road loomed, the perception began to spread that the opinion of the Board was leaning toward the Palm Canyon route. Because a decision on the route seemed very close, J. Win Wilson, together with the Associated Chambers of Commerce of the Coachella Valley, sprang into action, appearing before the Board of Supervisors at their regular meeting of September 23. At that meeting, Wilson "gave advance notice that within a short time [we] will flood the board with petitions bearing signatures of hundreds of persons asking that the Keen-Camp-to-the-Desert scenic road go via Pinon flats."[17]

For the next three weeks, Wilson and several other members of the Associated Chambers of Commerce of the Coachella Valley printed petitions and took them to Chamber meetings, civic organization meetings, and put them in drug stores throughout the Coachella Valley. "Have You Signed For Pinon Pines Road?" asked the Indio *Date Palm* of October 11, 1929. Wilson's goal was to have the petitions signed and delivered to the Board of Supervisors on October 14.

On that day, in the words of the San Jacinto Valley *Register*, a "monster petition for Pinon Road" was delivered to the Board.[18] Nearly 1,000 signatures had been collected by Wilson and his associates.[19] Bartlett Hayes, a banker and farmer from Indio, together with Walter Morgan, the owner of the La Quinta Hotel, filed the petitions with the Board, which also included ringing endorsements from almost every civic, service, and fraternal organization in the Coachella Valley. Calling the route a "public health step for the heat-ridden valley folks," Hayes indicated that were the route chosen, people in the valley could take the short drive into the mountains to escape the heat and return refreshed in the early morning for work. "When you take away a man's sleep, you have killed his efficiency, and for that reason this project is of tremendous importance to us of the valley. The Pinon Flats road would put the valley within a short drive of an elevation of 4,000 feet where the nights are cool. It is a public health proposition with us and we hope that the board will view our petition in that light. . . There is no controversy in the valley; we are a unit in urging your approval of the Pinon Flats route."[20]

This meeting of the Board of Supervisors gave much hope for the Pinyon Flats supporters. First, of course, was the submittal of the petitions which could only make a tremendous impression on the hearing body. After the petitions had been submitted and the Board went on to other business, Alexander Fulmor asked that $600 be appropriated for an aerial survey of the Pinon Flats route so that he could better secure the necessary information he needed for his upcoming report. The Board authorized the expenditure, and then went into a prolonged discussion of the potential of asking the federal government for assistance in building the road (federal involvement in the building of the Pines-to-Palms Highway will be examined further in Chapter 5). At this point, Wilson and his supporters had definitely made their position known, and the stage was set for a prolonged confrontation regarding the final route of the mountain-to-desert highway.[21]

Meanwhile, the other staunch supporter of the Pinyon Flats route was continuing his earlier, separate scheme. Wilson Howell Jr. was working to clear and develop most of the route from Vandeventer Flats through Pinyon Flats – the part of the route that was still somewhat undeveloped from the earlier attempts by himself and J. Win Wilson. During Fulmor's survey, Howell offered his knowledge of the area to Alex Fulmor and his crews as they surveyed the route proposed for Pinyon Flats. In fact, most of the route surveyed by Fulmor had already been laid out and partially improved by Howell. In the fall of 1929, Howell brought crews into the Pinyon Flats area to help clear his rudimentary road and make it suitable for drivers who were not as accustomed to driving through dense brush as he was. Wilson Howell was interviewed about his project, and he stated that:

Five miles of road have been built from the pavement between Indio and Palm Springs up a gentle slope to the base of the desert mountains, from there an old Indian trail covers four miles that the amateur road builders will not attempt to work on, as most of the distance is through rocky country, so those wishing to make the whole trip will have to walk the four miles. This is the only part of the route where any difficulty will be found in building the mountain-to-desert high-gear road and this will not be a serious obstacle to the county road crew with its efficient management and modern equipment.

Last year the scout car pushed its way through five miles of brush, trees and rocks and did not stop until it came to a canyon that no amount of driving and hand road building can conquer. This canyon is a tributary to Deep Canyon southeast of Black Hill and in it is a group of beautiful native palms with many other groups in the yawning depths of Deep Canyon and other tributary canyons. These groups of palms in no way equal the palms of Palm Canyon in number nor are they as accessible but viewed from the jutting points above, they add greatly to the scenic beauty of this wild rocky gorge with its 1200 to 1500 feet of depth, that offers grandeur entirely different from that of Palm Canyon, grandeur that the visitors will long remember.

The scout party walked down the trail where they were met by enthusiastic friends and escorted back to Indio after two days of struggle. Later they returned with help and worked over the tracks of the first trip and with repeated efforts the original tracks are becoming a road which any good mountain driver will enjoy traveling. The county engineer has completed a survey of a high gear road over this route.[22]

On October 28, 1929, support for the Pinyon Pines route gained more steam when additional petitions were given to the Board. These new petitions were signed mainly by residents of Thermal and Mecca. J. Win Wilson had followed up on his promise and obviously made his mark. At the same time, Alex Fulmor announced to the Board that the proposed West Fork of Palm Canyon route was completely infeasible. Citing potential costs of up to $50,000 per mile, Fulmor stated that,

> We traveled along a ridge between Murray and Palm Canyon, finding what is undoubtedly some of the roughest and brushiest country I've ever seen in the mountains. . . When we followed a grade line along the north side of the canyon so as to take advantage of as much sunshine as possible, to a view toward the problem winter snows would bring up, we found precipitous slopes of rock out of which a road would have to be blasted.[23]

With the announcement that Fulmor came out strongly against the West Fork route, attention focused squarely on the Palm Canyon and Pinyon Flats routes. All the parties involved could do now was to wait for the results of the survey. However, that didn't keep the supporters of the Pinyon Flats route from showing off Wilson Howell's handiwork. In November, they sponsored a barbecue at the foot of Dead Indian Canyon to emphasize their support for that route. People from Imperial County, Idyllwild, and of course the Coachella Valley were invited to inspect the route.[24] (One of these invitees was an unnamed member of one of the local womens' clubs, who wrote an editorial in the

80

Woman's Club Service Bulletin outlining Howell's road and the need for the Pinyon Flats route. This editorial is included as Appendix H).

Over the next several months, the rhetoric for and against the proposed routes subsided, only because all parties were still awaiting the results of Alex Fulmor's detailed survey. That survey, however, was delayed several times. Originally, it was to have been submitted around the end of October, 1929. December 1929 was the next target date, followed by the end of 1929. When that didn't materialize, January and then February, 1930 were the next announcements of the submission of the survey.

By the time February 1930 arrived, two new twists had come about that seemed to shore up the routing of the new road down the Pinyon Flats route. At a meeting of the Palm Springs Chamber of Commerce (one of the groups that had sponsored the request for the road up Palm Canyon a year before), the group discussed the two routes again and voted unanimously to endorse the Pinyon Flats route for the road. Sentiment was beginning to change in Palm Springs, and many did not want to see Palm Canyon altered in any way by putting a road through it. Palm Canyon was too important a tourist destination to grade the sides of the canyon for a highway:

> It does seem a shame, in fact it is tragic, to think of further exploiting beautiful Palm Canyon by putting a road through it and thus marring its beauty beyond repair. If there is one place in California which should be left as near as possible in its natural state, that place is Palm Canyon, and it is to be hoped that the many residents of Palm Springs who feel likewise will make themselves heard before it is too late.[25]

This revelation, of course, was greeted warmly by J. Win Wilson and other supporters of the Pinyon Flats route.[26] The

Hemet *News* touted the change by the Palm Springs Chamber by saying that "this action is believed to mark the abandonment of all organized effort to route the new highway down Palm Canyon."[27] Furthermore, Newton Drury, the acquisitions officer for California State Parks, expressed serious concerns himself, having seen what automobile highways had done in the redwood regions of the state:

> I am somewhat fearful that the National Park Service will be maneuvered into the position we have found ourselves in as regards the redwoods; namely, approval of highway routings on the assumption that there will be no material damage to the landscape etc. etc. only to find later that we have been a party more or less to an appalling debacle which with less hast and more plans could in many respects have been avoided... I even... express the inclination to believe that any high speed road on modern highway standards through a scenic area [is] to be considered as nothing less than a misfortune.[28]

The second item to bolster the cause of the Pinyon Flats route was the February 18th release of preliminary numbers by Alex Fulmor showing that route to be the least expensive of the three routes surveyed. As indicated several months before, a rough estimate of the West Fork route was between $900,000 and $1,000,000 – well outside of the amount of money the Board wanted to spend or could spend on such a road. Fulmor estimated that the Palm Canyon route would cost approximately $504,600 and entail moving 600,000 cubic yards of dirt, whereas the Pinyon Flats route would cost approximately $361,900 while moving only 400,000 cubic yards.[29]

With the strong amount of continued support for the Pinyon Flats route from the Coachella Valley, the revelation that the Palm Springs Chamber of Commerce no longer wanted the road to lead through Palm Canyon, and the preliminary cost estimates from the County Surveyor showing the Pinyon Flats route to be the least expensive, it must have seemed that the controversy was over except for the formal decision by the Board of Supervisors. As it turned out, though, the story was about to take yet another turn.

On March 3, the Riverside County Board of Supervisors received a letter from Dr. George Clements, a leading member of the Los Angeles Chamber of Commerce and a strong proponent of the push to create Mt. San Jacinto State Park. In the letter, he described the necessity of the road and of the State Park, but admonished the Riverside County officials for considering two routes when Los Angeles officials assumed from the beginning that the proposed road would go to Palm Springs via Palm Canyon. In the words of Dr. Clements, the potential for a route besides the Palm Canyon route was "rather a surprise to us, as we believed that the route of this road had been fairly well established prior to the establishment of the mountain park project; that it was to follow the Palm canyon route and thus make available that particular portion of the Coachella valley which must be considered from all angles as the only reason for the contemplation of such a road."[30] There had already been widespread discussions that Los Angeles County may be willing to contribute $50,000 toward an enlargement of Mt. San Jacinto State Park, and that would be in jeopardy if the Riverside County Board chose the Pinyon Flats route.

Riverside County Board Chairman Thorndike Jameson, a constant supporter for a mountain-to-desert road but always leery of the cost, made the letter public and announced that it was his intention to ask that the two Boards of Supervisors hold a meeting to discuss forming a joint road district for the purposes of constructing the mountain-to-desert road. Arthur Lovekin, the president of the Mt. San Jacinto State Park Association, joined in this call indicating that the building of the road and the possible formation of a State Park were coterminous. "The construction of the road is a matter vital to the park . . . The park itself will be the greatest natural asset in Southern California and the road as proposed for construction under a joint district would serve as the eastern gateway."[31] Supervisor Jameson got his wish when the Board voted to postpone a decision on the route and attempt to enter into negotiations with Los Angeles County.[32]

The reasons behind this new attempt to work in conjunction with Los Angeles County were many. First, most of the visitors to Palm Canyon and the neighboring area were from Los Angeles. Therefore, it was felt by several people that Los Angeles should have a stake in both the creation of a park and also, potentially, a road to get there for its citizens. Secondly, the road to Palm Canyon was a dead-end road, and the traffic situation on it was becoming desperate as more and more visitors thronged to the area. On the weekend of March 1-2, 1930, a Captain King of the California Highway Patrol counted fully 36,000 cars passing the "Y" in Beaumont, many of them coming from the desert.[33] As a supplement to this count, another officer under Captain King's command counted fully 500 vehicles driving into Palm Canyon before 11:30 a.m. on Sunday March 2. The road from Palm Springs to Palm Canyon had no outlet, and there were serious implications of having that much traffic use a dead-end road. Captain King reported that:

The Beaumont "Y" circa 1940. View is looking to the southeast.
(Photo courtesy Gary McKenzie)

> The congestion became so great we were forced to establish a station a considerable distance down the canyon, permitting no more cars to pass that point than were coming out . . . In this way we kept the 'bench' filled all the time. We heard many complaints to the condition and motorists hardly without exception did not take well to being stopped, but had we let them go on into the canyon, they probably would have been there yet.[34]

Third, despite the fact that just a few weeks previous to the March 3 Board meeting, the Palm Springs Chamber of Commerce had endorsed the Pinyon Flats route, many of the business and hotel owners in Palm Springs were upset and ready to make a further pitch for the Palm Canyon route:

> Coincident with the board's action, it became known that the Palm Springs interests . . . are preparing a determined campaign to convince Palm Springs of the asserted error of allowing the road to avoid Palm Canyon. Leaders of the movement there understood to include several of the most prominent property owners and hotel proprietors.[35]

The final reason for the delay was Dr. Clements himself, who was now in the thick of the attempt to create a State park. Dr. Clements' comments seemed to have quite a bit of validity, and so with his letter addressing the Riverside County Board, the Board members naturally thought that this was more than a passing overture by Los Angeles County to see that the mountain-to-desert road was built. Clements reasoned that the Palm Canyon route would be closer to Los Angeles and alleviate the growing traffic problem, whereas the Pinyon Flats route "would diverge from [a] wilderness area and follow through a comparatively bleak desert region with no beauty any way comparable with the famous Palm Canyon scenery."[36] With all of the aforementioned reasons, and the hope that Riverside County would not have to foot the bill for the entire new road, it was natural that the Board of Supervisors would postpone further work on the route in the hope that negotiations could lead to a joint effort.

The Riverside *Enterprise* said of this new twist that "the entire complexion of the San Jacinto Mountains to Desert Highway is altered . . . [the] Pinyon Flats route is apparently about due for discard."[37] With support from Los Angeles, it was reasoned, it may be possible to obtain State funding to help build the road, since it was to be a scenic route. Projections were that up to one half the cost of the road could be paid by the State, with the other half borne by both Los Angeles and Riverside Counties. Despite the fact that Alex Fulmor's numbers were showing that construction of the Pinyon Flats route would be the cheaper of the two main routes, having the State and Los Angeles County pay upwards of 75% of the cost of the Palm Canyon route naturally would have been the most cost-effective means for Riverside County.

This new twist by the Board naturally brought a vehement and animated response from J. Win Wilson and the other Coachella Valley supporters of the Pinyon Flats route. At a mass showing of support for the Pinyon Flats route at the Board meeting of March 17, 1930, which included the presentation of a large number of signed letters all in support of the Pinyon Flats route, Bartlett Hayes came out and asked the Board directly if they had changed their attitude toward the road and their desert constituents. An offended Supervisor Jameson indicated that no decision had been made or would be until all the information was in. Hayes then asked the Board to vote on the Pinyon Flats route, which they refused. The Board did promise the Coachella Valley people that a decision would be made on April 7 and that they would be given at least 2 weeks' notice of the meeting. Supervisor John Shaver then made a motion to begin construction on the Pinyon Flats route while negotiations continued, but it lost on lack of a second.[38] Hayes reiterated the many reasons for choosing the Pinyon

Flats route, wherein Supervisor Jameson told the crowd that there was a chance that both routes could be constructed:

> Provided the county of Riverside can pay one-third, the county of Los Angeles one-third and the state will appropriate the remainder, under a joint-county road district as proposed for the Palm canyon road, the board would certainly be justified in taking up this proposition, which would be cheaper to the county than constructing the Pinon Flats route. . . . I would say that if we can get a joint road district for the construction of the Palm canyon route, and then build a road by prison camp labor over the Pinon Flats route, perhaps not so expensive a road as has been outlined by the county surveyor, that would be my choice.[39]

By the end of the meeting, after several lengthy speeches, the Board adjourned and all went back to their respective locations to await, yet again, the report by Fulmor and the response (if any) from the Los Angeles Board.

Fulmor's eagerly-awaited complete report was finally submitted to the Board on March 10 (it had been scheduled for March 3, but was postponed due to the newest turn of events). These of course were the final survey results and recommendations for the three routes. In a lengthy presentation, Fulmor outlined the pros and cons of all three routes, their projected costs, and the length of time estimated to construct each of them. Citing concerns such as the ability of the road to open areas for recreational use, the closeness of the mountains to the greatest number of Coachella Valley residents, and the sheer amount of work that would be involved in constructing each of the three routes, Fulmor concluded that the Pinyon Flats route was definitely his choice for the road (Fulmor's full report, summarized in the Indio *Date Palm* with pros and cons for each of the routes, is reproduced as Appendix I).

Fulmor's report only served to strengthen the call for the Pinyon Flats route, but with the potential for involvement by Los Angeles County, enthusiasm over Fulmor's results was tempered. To see if there was any true support in Los Angeles for the Palm Canyon road, J. Win Wilson addressed a letter to Sidney Graves, the acting Chair of the Los Angeles County Board of Supervisors, asking him whether the Los Angeles Board was truly behind the project. Graves responded that "Los Angeles County is not interested in the proposed road up Palm Canyon in Riverside County. There may be individuals here who are interested in the matter but they in no way represent the official attitude of this Board of Supervisors."[40] This letter was presented to the Riverside County Board on April 7, with the Board only indicating that a final decision would not be made before April 21.[41]

The final piece to the very tangled puzzle of where the mountain-to-desert road would ultimately lead came from a group that had heretofore not been mentioned in any of the accounts or arguments related to the controversy. In advocating for the Palm Canyon route, few if any proponents seem to have paid any attention to the fact that Palm Canyon and its environs were part of the Agua Caliente Indian Reservation, and thus controlled by the Agua Caliente people.[42] In April 1930, officials from Riverside County approached the Agua Caliente regarding securing a right-of-way for the proposed road. This request was unequivocally turned down. As officials with Riverside County and the Bureau of Indian Affairs continued to push the Agua Caliente Indians for either ownership of or a lease of Palm Canyon, the Agua Caliente pushed back harder. After about six weeks, it was noted that the Agua Caliente had begun fencing their property in the vicinity of Palm Canyon with the intention of closing the road and charging a toll for entrance into Palm Canyon. The fence was being erected for two reasons – first, as evidenced by CHP Captain King's report of a few months before, too many visitors and tourists were coming to Palm Canyon, creating a traffic hazard and leaving the natural wonder in a severe state of disrepair. Rod McKenzie, the county's road superintendent, indicated that these visitors "have left so much trash, including papers and empty lunch boxes, that the roadsides resemble a city dump instead of a mountain park."[43] The second reason for the fence was to contain the Agua Caliente cattle, which heretofore had been allowed to roam freely between the checkerboard holdings of the tribe, but were now the object of scorn within the growing town of Palm Springs.[44] For some time previous, residents of Palm Springs, angry about the Agua Caliente's horses and cattle roaming the streets at will, began impounding the animals. This naturally angered the Agua Caliente people. Throughout May and June, a few attempts were made to assuage them, but to no avail. The specter of Riverside County having to force the issue of putting a road up Palm Canyon and through the reservation in light of the problems the Agua Caliente people faced was simply too much.

At the regular meeting of the Riverside County Board of Supervisors on July 21, 1930, discussion again focused on the route of the mountain to desert road. Abruptly, Supervisor John Shaver, who had long been a proponent of the Pinyon Flat route, made a motion to adopt the Pinyon Flats route, stating that "there is no other action for us to take . . . for it will save us more than $100,000 and is the logical route." Supervisor Harvey Johnson seconded the motion, and when it came to a vote, the motion passed unanimously. After 24 months, several hearings, and several hundreds of hours spent by supporters in bolstering their cases, the Board of Supervisors decided that the county's new road that would do so much to further the reputation and tourist industry of Riverside County, would lead from Keen Camp to Vandeventer Flats, and then to the desert below via Pinyon Flats and the Dead Indian Canyon. Less than a month after the final decision on the route, the Board gave the new road its official name – the Pines-to-Palms Highway.[45]

Chapter 3 Notes

1. The road from Palm Springs to Palm Canyon had been improved as early as 1925. Palm Canyon had already been a tourist destination for many years, offering a place to hike, picnic, and explore.

2. This latter route had already been laid out by Wilson Howell (Quinn, 2011).

3. In short, it would go along the ridge that is today the Seven Level Hill.

4. This turn to the east is essentially what is Apple Canyon Road today near the entrance to Hurkey Creek Park.

5. Both of these peaks were unnamed at the time of the building of the Pines-to-Palms Highway. In fact, the area hadn't even been surveyed for section boundaries according to Alex Fulmor's 1929 and 1936 maps of Riverside County. The peaks were probably named in the 1960s. Spitler Peak is named for George Spitler, an early settler who built a ranch at the head of Fobes Creek in the 1880s only to later discover that the land was previously claimed by Charles Thomas, who drove him out (Bill Sapp, Forest Archaeologist for the San Bernardino National Forest, personal e-mail communication with the author, August 2, 2011). Nothing could be found about the naming of Apache Peak.

6. The exact location of this proposed route is not known. No precise description of it was ever given, probably because it was a minor proposal. I have tried to ascertain what may have been the route based upon examination of aerial photos and the brief descriptions in the contemporary record.

7. Alternately, it could have gone up a slightly lower ridge between Apache Peak and Antsell Rock.

8. Indio *Date Palm*, March 16, 1928.

9. Retention of the prison camp in the mountains was another point brought up by Boyd and the others. There were many moves afoot to relocate the prison camp to construct some of the other roads under consideration at this time.

10. Riverside County Board of Supervisors Minutes, March 11, 1929, Banning *Record*, March 14, 1929.

11. Although this may seem redundant because of the earlier surveys, this new survey was to be more detail-oriented and also include the pros and cons of each route plus also Fulmor's recommendations based upon his engineering background.

12. Riverside County Board of Supervisors Minutes, March 25, 1929; Indio *Date Palm*, March 29, 1929.

13. Indio *Date Palm*, March 29, 1929.

14. Banning *Record*, April 4, 1929; Indio *Date Palm*, April 5, 1929. Plans for this tour were hastily made because the parties hoped for a quick decision, and also it was spring – with summer not too far beyond.

15. It is obvious that this tour was more than a sight-seeing excursion by the Board of Supervisors. Several important people with ties to the San Jacinto Mountain area and the State of California accompanied the Board to view the possibilities of the proposed road. Members of the group included:

    Riverside County Supervisors Thorndike C. Jameson, John Shaver, Harvey Johnson, John E. McGregor, and William C. Moore
    Alexander Fulmor, Riverside County Surveyor
    Albert E. Bottel – Riverside County Horticultural Commissioner and Secretary of the San Jacinto Mountain State Park Association
    Emanuel T. Mische – California State Parks Commissioner (Mische was a renowned park designer. He was a protégé of John Charles Olmsted (step-son of Frederick Law Olmstead) and had designed several parks in Portland, Oregon).
    Unnamed representative of Frederick Law Olmsted
    F. E. Bonner, district engineer U. S. Department of Forestry
    Fred J. Grumm, engineer with the California Division of Highways
    John E. Elliot, U. S. Forest Service supervisor for San Bernardino
    Ernest E. East, Chief Engineer with the Automobile Club of Southern California
    Elwood C. Wickerd, Superintendent of the Riverside County Prison Camps
    Mr. and Mrs. Claudius Lee Emerson of Idyllwild, Incorporated
    Jessica Bird, Riverside Daily *Press*
    John Winfield Wilson, Indio *Date Palm*
    Several members of the Banning, Palm Springs, Coachella, Thermal, and Indio Chambers of Commerce, and representatives of the Indio Lions Club, Indio Exchange Club, American Legion, Indio Womens' Club, Coachella Valley Farm Bureau, Coachella Valley Water District, and the Deglet Noor Date Growers' Association (Riverside Daily *Press*, April 18, 1929, Indio *Date Palm*, April 19, 1929).

16. Indio *Date Palm*, April 5, 1929.

17. Indio *Date Palm*, September 27, 1929.

18. San Jacinto Valley *Register*, October 24, 1929. The Banning *Record*

19. of October 24, 1929, indicated that it was the longest petition in Riverside County history.

20. To put this in perspective, the 1930 census listed 3,484 persons in Indio township, where most if not all of the signatures would have been gathered. The unincorporated town of Palm Springs was not included in the Indio township – it was included in the San Gorgonio township, together with Beaumont, Banning, Cabazon, and Whitewater. The population of San Gorgonio Township in 1930 was 1,943. (United States Federal Census Data, 1930).

21. Bartlett Hayes' comments to the Riverside County Board of Supervisors, October 14, 1929, as quoted in the San Jacinto Valley *Register*, October 24, 1929 and the Hemet *News*, October 25, 1929. Curiously, the fight for the Pinyon Flats route had by this time become one of public health and not solely economics as it was in the beginning. Perhaps the citizens of the lower Coachella Valley believed their arguments would have more traction with the Board if they touted the "public health" angle instead of merely the economic angle.

22. During this meeting, Board Chairman Thorndike Jameson indicated that the decision of the route may be based heavily upon cost. Hayes responded to him by asking that a road not be built through Palm Canyon which would mar the scenery and disrupt the groves of palm trees therein (Banning *Record*, October 24, 1929).

23. Hemet *News*, September 27, 1929.

24. Los Angeles *Times*, October 30, 1929. $50,000 per mile would have been quite a steep price. By contrast, most everyone at this time estimated the entire mountain-to-desert road to cost $500,000 for approximately 35 miles. This averages approximately $14,300 per mile. At $50,000 per mile, the West Fork of Palm Canyon route would cost approximately $1,000,000 to build.

25. Indio *Date Palm*, November 8, 1929.

26. Editorial by the Indio *News*, quoted in the Riverside *Press*, March 19, 1930.

27. Indio *Date Palm*, February 7, 1930.

28. Hemet *News*, February 7, 1930.

29. Drury, Newton, letter to Frederick Law Olmsted Jr., May 1, 1930. At this time, Drury was the acquisitions officer for the California State Department of Natural Resources, Division of Parks. Drury was a very influential person in both California and National park history, and would eventually broker the deal to create Mt. San Jacinto State

Park. Newton Drury Peak, just southwest of Mt. San Jacinto peak, was named for him.

29. Indio *Date Palm*, February 21, 1930 and March 28, 1930.
30. Hemet *News*, March 7, 1930.
31. Hemet *News*, March 7, 1930.
32. Los Angeles *Times*, March 4, 1930. The *Times* called the move by the Riverside County Board an "unusual proposal."
33. This Y, in present-day terms, is roughly where State Route 60 splits from the I-10 freeway in Beaumont. At the time, the 60-70-99 highway led from Beaumont northwest toward Redlands, and the Jackrabbit Trail heading to the San Jacinto Valley split from it at the Y.
34. Riverside *Enterprise*, March 4, 1930.
35. Riverside *Enterprise*, March 4, 1930.
36. Los Angeles *Times*, March 4, 1930.
37. Riverside *Enterprise*, March 4, 1930.
38. Hemet *News*, March 21, 1930.
39. Indio *Date Palm*, March 21, 1930.
40. Indio *Date Palm*, April 4, 1930. This potential turn of events on the part of Los Angeles County was not so. The letter received by the Board on March 3 by Dr. Clements had been construed to be an official letter. It was not. In fact, it was Dr. Clements making one last plea for his own benefit. Dr. Clements had been one of the leaders pushing for the formation of either a National Park or National Monument for Palm Canyon in 1919. He led a small group of wealthy people who had purchased land around Palm Canyon during the push to make it a park or monument. As it came to light later, there were many interests who wanted to develop resort hotels in the area. By 1930, Clements still owned his property in the vicinity, and wanted to cash in on a scenic highway going right near or alongside his land. The fact that the Los Angeles County Board of Supervisors answered J. Win Wilson so frankly speaks volumes about their relationship with Dr. Clements. (For an in-depth discussion of this part of the episode, see Davis, pp 49-54).
41. Indio *Date Palm*, April 11, 1930.
42. This probably had more to do with the fact that obtaining road right-of-way in those days, especially in outlying areas and for the public good, was almost assured. People who advocated for the Palm Canyon road probably believed that obtaining the necessary route would be a small matter of negotiations with the Bureau of Indian Affairs, and

43. Indio *Date Palm*, May 29, 1930. It will be remembered by the modern reader that Tahquitz Canyon, another part of the Agua Caliente Reservation, was closed for several years for the same reason.

44. Indio *Date Palm*, June 6, 1930. An editorial in the San Bernardino *Sun,* quoted in the Indio *Date Palm* of June 6, 1930, summed up many peoples' feelings well:

> Certain interests over in the Whitewater valley rise to protest because the Indians are fencing a portion of their reservation that includes Palm canyon. The winter colony of Palm Springs protested against the presence of grazing cattle in its streets. The Indians have a right of use at the famous desert community's spring so when their cattle were not wanted they promptly began fencing off their reservation boundary. That the fence crossed an undedicated road up Palm canyon where picnic parties had trespassed for a generation or more did not bother the Indian. It is even intimated that the tribal finances may be enhanced by the erection of a toll gate on the Palm canyon road. The Indians have apparently taken a leaf from the white man's book for they are reported to have consulted Federal District Attorney McNabb before acting and to have received assurance that the toll road proposition is within their rights. . . . How much the action of the Indians has to do with the road routing battle may be a question. The growth of Palm Springs and winter tourist business has hampered stock-raising on the nearby reservation. Tourist parties have littered the scenic canyons with paper cups, tin cans, et cetera, until an observer cannot blame the Indians for becoming incensed and fencing off his reservation.

45. Riverside County Board of Supervisors Minutes, August 11, 1930; Los Angeles *Times*, August 13, 1930. Efforts to put a road down Palm Canyon would continue for a few months, but to no avail. It was hoped that building both roads would make a scenic loop route benefiting both Palm Springs and the rest of the Coachella Valley. Funding sources dried up, and the Agua Caliente continued to refuse to give up ownership of Palm Canyon. With this, the issue was effectively dead.

Chapter 4
Early Construction and More Route Problems

While the controversy over which route the road would eventually take raged on, actual construction on what would become the Pines-to-Palms Highway began with little fanfare. On August 15, 1929, it was announced that work on the Hemet-Idyllwild road would be completed within 30 days. Since the Board had already approved the new road in concept using the existing prison road crew, Elwood Wickerd, the county's prison road camp superintendent, believed that within 60 days, the prison camp crews, then numbering about 55 inmates, could be shifted over to begin work on the "Keen Camp-Palm Springs" road. This despite the fact that Alex Fulmor and his crews still had approximately six months of work ahead of them surveying the three routes proposed for the road. The ability to start on the new road, however, was due to the fact that the first six miles, from the existing new highway to Herkey Creek, was to be the same no matter which route was chosen.[1]

The actual date construction began is unknown. There was no grand ceremony to mark a groundbreaking event. In all likelihood, sometime in September 1929, Elwood Wickerd began shifting men from the completion of the Hemet-Idyllwild road to the beginning of the road to the desert. Because this portion of the proposed road already existed to a great extent, it was generally believed that construction would progress rapidly. By October 7, Alex Fulmor could tell the Board that two miles of the new road had already been constructed.[2]

Fulmor's announcement at the end of October that the West Fork of Palm Canyon route was completely infeasible meant that construction could progress beyond Herkey Creek and toward Vandeventer Flat. Therefore, negotiations were opened with the Lake Hemet Water District and the Garner family for rights-of-way through most of the Garner Valley.[3] Throughout the late fall of 1929, actual construction work tapered off due to the weather, the need to secure the right-of-way, and the need to design and construct bridges to cross Herkey Creek and a few others found throughout the Garner Valley. By the time 1930 began, it was noted that the number of inmates at the prison camp was expected to swell to over 100 as Riverside County witnessed its own crime wave. As the effects of the stock market crash of the previous October were beginning to be felt hard throughout the nation, crime was on the increase, and Riverside County was poised to take advantage of a larger number of inmates for its road building.[4]

On January 6, 1930, Elwood Wickerd reported that the first three miles of the road were completed and that the advance crews using a steam shovel were within 350 feet of Herkey Creek. At the same time, the announcement was made that the right-of-way for the road across the property of the Lake Hemet Water Company had been secured, and condemnation proceedings could start.[5] Apparently the thought of using the prison crews to construct bridges over the creeks was dismissed at this point. On January 20, 1930, the Board authorized Alex Fulmor to develop plans and specifications for the bridges and prepare to bid the work. He did, and the construction of bridges was advertised for bid. On March 3, the bids were opened and none of the bids were found to be satisfactory, so the Board authorized the county's Road Department to construct them.[6]

By mid-January, the prison crews were taken off the new road due to the construction of the Herkey Creek bridge (the large steam shovel they were using could not cross the creek) and the right-of-way negotiations. They were sent to do additional work on the Hemet-Idyllwild road which included cutting back some sharp turns and preparing the road for an oil seal that the federal government was going to place on the road. Crews would not start work again on the Pines-to-Palms road until summer.

Bridge construction work continued through the spring and summer, with the bridges being completed around August 1, 1930. At that point, the pace of road construction could increase due to the fact that most of the road was going along relatively flat ground.[7] Although the old two-track road through Garner Valley led along the northeastern side of the valley, the new road would be straighter and hug the southwestern side.[8]

Throughout the spring of 1930, as the survey progressed and construction of the bridges continued, one major landowner to the south came to the forefront of the quest for rights-of-way. The "all roads are good" attitude that generally prevailed among white residents of the area did not necessarily extend to the Santa Rosa Indians. They read the papers too and talked to the workers and knew that the road was heading toward their reservation, and in fact would have to cross it to get through Vandeventer Flats. The estimate from Fulmor was that four miles of right-of-way would have to be secured along the northern portion of the reservation for the road.[9] With that knowledge, and the fact that apparently no one had contacted the Santa Rosas beforehand to discuss a right-of-way, a delegation from the reservation appeared at the Board's meeting of April 7, 1930, asking what the county's intention

The Riverside County Road Camp, early 1930s.
(Photo courtesy Jim Wickerd)

*(Top) Elwood Wickerd at the Dripping Springs road camp, early-mid 1930s.
(Bottom) Lunch time at the Dripping Springs road camp, early-mid 1930s.
Although not taken at the Pines-to-Palms road camp, these photos show views
of a camp that would not have been much different than the mountain camp.
(Photos courtesy Jim Wickerd)*

Garner Valley from the Pines-to-Palms Highway

was. At that time, the Board directed that a meeting be held between the Santa Rosas and Alex Fulmor to discuss the routing of the road.[10] The assumption on the county's part that they could secure a right-of-way across the Santa Rosa Reservation would be the next big controversy to plague the Pines-to-Palms Highway.

After Fulmor met with the Santa Rosas, a formal meeting for negotiation was called.[11] At this meeting between the Santa Rosas and the Board, the Board offered $1,000 for the right-of-way. The Santa Rosas, led by Alex Tortes, scoffed at the offer and left. They returned to their homes and appealed to the Bureau of Indian Affairs in Washington, D.C. to intercede. Charles Ellis, the Mission Indian agent in the area, met with the Santa Rosas and was informed that they would hold out for $8,000 for the right-of-way, and were prepared to block construction of the road if necessary. They needed the money to develop wells and an irrigation system on their land, and saw this as a perfect opportunity to get the funds.

On August 11, the Santa Rosas' demands were presented to the Board by Ellis, setting the stage for a months-long showdown between the two parties. The road crews were getting closer to the reservation each day. It was estimated that construction crews would reach the western boundary line of the reservation in approximately four months. "If a right of way has not been legally secured by that time, an embarrassing situation may develop, officials fear."[12]

In response to the demands of the Santa Rosas, the Board hired former Supervisor Thomas Flaherty, a real estate broker and appraiser, to develop a valuation for the land. In Flaherty's opinion, $495 was a "liberal amount for the land desired by the county as the right of way across the reservation," and scoffed at the Indians' demand for $8,000. With that information, the Board decided to compile a dossier of Flaherty's appraisal, along with some neighboring appraisals and tax valuations, and send all of the information to both the Bureau of Indian Affairs and Congressman Phil Swing to help bolster the county's position.[13]

Both sides now seem to have solidified their positions and were unwilling to budge. Meanwhile, others were trying to secure alternatives to the standoff. One idea that came to light was to reroute the road around the reservation. That would have meant a longer road with greater costs for redesign and construction, plus a delay due to the extra engineering work. Another idea was to pay the Santa Rosas something extra for the tillable lands that were to be taken up within the right-of-way. In the meantime, Wickerd's construction crews kept getting closer to the reservation, being about two months' away by one estimate in the beginning of September, 1930.[14]

At this point, not eager to see his beloved road delayed for this or any other reason, J. Win Wilson approached the Board and offered to mediate the situation. The Board authorized him to meet with the Santa Rosas regarding a lesser subsidy for the right-of-way. Wilson was able to secure a promise from the Santa Rosas to accept a payment of $4,000, but he obviously felt that the county was taking a heavy hand in dealings with both them and the Agua Caliente Indians at Palm Canyon:

THE INDIANS DO HAVE RIGHTS

. . . We are again forcibly reminded that the Indian reservations "do not belong to us." The Date Palm has called attention to this little technicality many times in years past, but very few appeared to understand it.

Now the Palm Springs Indians are actually going to put a toll gate at the entrance of Palm Canyon, and the Indian agent, Mr. C. L. Ellis, has so informed the board of supervisors. It may as well be understood right now that the rights of condemnation do not obtain against the Indians and the usual "strong-arm" methods of the white man are of no avail. The high-handed policy of the board of supervisors in trying to deal with the Indians is at fault. The Indians are not to be rushed off their feet by any such methods.

At the personal suggestion of the chairman of the board of supervisors, the writer has made two trips to the Van Deventer Flats and obtained from the Indians a modified demand – a reduction from $8,000 to $4,000 for a right of way for the Pines-to-Palms road, and it is our opinion that the board had better accept this proposal before the Indians have time to change their minds.[15]

By the middle of September, 1930, cooler heads were beginning to prevail and a meeting was called between the parties. On September 14, Alex Fulmor, Charles Ellis, Samuel Cary Evans, J. Win Wilson and Wilson Howell met with members of the Santa Rosa Tribe on the reservation to discuss the situation and see if there could be a mutual understanding. This meeting proved very fruitful. Because the actual layout of the road had changed a few times over the previous months, the Santa Rosas had been under the mistaken impression about the final, approved route. Once Alex Fulmor showed them the true adopted line for the highway according to his plans, they were in agreement that the impact would not be as great as they had assumed, and they reaffirmed their pledge to accept the $4,000 subsidy negotiated by J. Win Wilson for the right-of-way.[16]

The Santa Rosas then turned attention to their concerns relative to their water needs. A large storm in 1927 had washed through much of their meadow and farm lands and had dropped the level of underground water nearly 20 feet. Their shallow wells were no longer producing water, and they were having to carry water from a creek. Many of their orchards were dying, and the Santa Rosas were becoming desperate for a solution. J. Win Wilson put it succinctly: ". . . the time to get their water conditions restored is when the white man wants a right of way across his land."

The Board, however, was standing firm on an offer of $1,240, which had increased slightly over the previous weeks from the original $1,000. The Board was trying to rush a right-of-way permit through the Bureau of Indian Affairs and waiting to hear from Washington D. C. regarding the matter. It was pointed out, though, by Charles Ellis that a special act of Congress would need to be made before the Bureau could act in this situation. Meanwhile, the construction crews were getting closer to the line of the reservation, the Santa Rosas were becoming more desperate for water, and many people were calling for the $4,000 payment to be made so that the road could be built and the Santa Rosas could get the water system they so desperately needed.[17]

A tentative break in the stalemate came during the Board's meeting on October 6. Word was received that the Santa Rosa Indians had submitted a formal protest over the dealings with Riverside County to the Bureau of Indian Affairs in Washington D. C. Commissioner Rhoads of the Bureau indicated that at that point no further decisions could be made until the protest was considered and a formal report made. Needless to say, this would cause a delay that could last for months. By this time, Wickerd reported that his crews were within two miles of the Santa Rosa Reservation boundary (about three weeks' work), and were not easing up on the construction timetable per direction from the Board. Fully twelve miles of the road had been built and the crews were making excellent progress through the flatter areas.[18] With the Santa Rosas holding firm on their demand for $4,000, and construction crews almost ready to begin crossing the boundary, there was little else the Board could do but indicate that they would be willing to consider moving their offer closer to the Indians' demand of $4,000 to avoid the lengthy delay.[19]

Sometime during the next week, the Board sent a letter to Commissioner Rhoads advising him that they would pay the $4,000 for the right-of-way provided that permission to cross the reservation could be secured within three weeks' time so that there would be no delay in construction. Rhoads responded by saying that the Santa Rosas were willing to oblige, and on October 20, the Board authorized payment of $4,000 to the Santa Rosa Indians for the right-of-way across their reservation.[20] This was met with a conditional approval

Boundary of the Santa Rosa Indian Reservation from the west. It was here that a potential showdown was averted.

to cross contingent upon payment. The only thing left to do was issue the check and sign the approval. All of the players in this episode gave a sigh of relief, but none moreso than Elwood Wickerd – on the same day the Board authorized the payment, his crews were only about a day and a half away from the boundary of the reservation. The stalemate had been broken just in time.[21]

Up to the time the stalemate was broken, construction of the road progressed at a rapid pace. That changed abruptly, though, because during the period when negotiations were being held, none of Wickerd's survey crews had been allowed access to the right-of-way through the Santa Rosa Reservation. The construction crews were forced to slow their pace for the next month while the surveyors went ahead to stake the route of the road. By December 8, it was reported that the construction crews had finished the first mile of roadway through the reservation, and were approximately 15 miles east of Keen Camp.[22]

Throughout the winter of 1930-1931, construction of the road continued at a rather rapid pace. By this time, the stated goal of the County of Riverside was to have the prison road camp crews construct the Pines-to-Palms Highway to Mile 22, and then have the federal government construct the rest

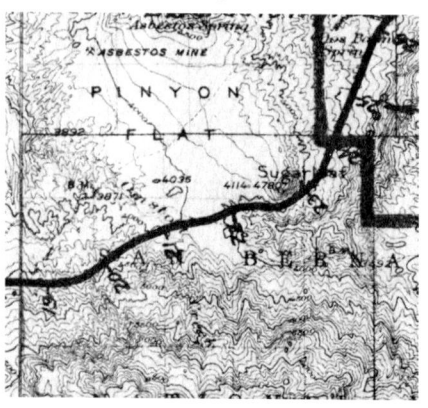

Map showing mileage along the proposed Pines-to-Palms Highway. Mile 22 is approximately the location where the highway crosses Onstott Creek. (Photo courtesy National Archives and Records Administration)

of the road leading from Mile 22 to the Palm Springs-Indio Highway.[23] At the Board's meeting of February 9, Elwood Wickerd could report that his crews had graded the road through the Santa Rosa Reservation and were busy on a bridge at the head of Palm Canyon.[24]

When the end of February arrived, another potential snag developed. In the four months since the Board of Supervisors made payment to the Bureau of Indian Affairs for the right-of-way, none of the money had been disbursed to the Santa Rosas. On February 23, the Board, together with Charles Ellis, began sending telegrams to the Bureau hoping to spur the release of funds to the Santa Rosas for their use. Bureau officials, however, indicated that they would disburse the money equally among all members of the tribe. Alex Tortes, leader and spokesman for the Santa Rosas, asked repeatedly to have the money given to the group as a whole so that the water system could be developed. Since at this time the road had been completed across the reservation, and the crews were working around the Mile 18 mark, the Santa Rosas threatened to bar traffic from using the road. They were assured that every effort would be made to secure their funds, and also that the county had a legal right-of-way which could not now be revoked.[25] With construction crews at the Mile 18 mark, only four miles of county-sponsored construction remained. Due to the nature of the territory and the greater amount of excavation needed in the area, Elwood Wickerd estimated that he and his "enrollees" would still be on the job for about 4-5 months.

At this time, it looked like the new highway would be mired in another controversy as the Santa Rosas, the County of Riverside, and several members of the community lobbied for the release of the $4,000 payment to the Santa Rosas. It was soon brought to light that the Bureau of Indian Affairs had taken the $4,000 payment by the Board of Supervisors and placed it in a fund to be doled out for the benefit of the Santa Rosas as Congress and the Bureau saw fit. This discovery made things worse for everyone in the region, because the Santa Rosas were left trying to untangle a web of red tape to get their due funds, and others who had backed the desire of the Santa Rosas to have the money for their own needs believed that Washington was meddling in local affairs. The Board of Supervisors asked District Attorney Earl Redwine to send a letter to Congressman Phil Swing requesting that he intercede on behalf of the Santa Rosas, while several community members, area residents, Indian rights activists, and newspapers were pressuring the Bureau to give the Santa Rosas the money that was rightfully theirs. This pressure finally had the desired effect. On April 13, 1931, it was announced that the Bureau would release the money to the Santa Rosas, but only on a pro-rata basis, since many of the approximately 50 members did not actually live on the reservation.[26] The Santa Rosas reluctantly agreed.

Throughout the spring of 1931, construction continued and the end of the county's portion of the highway was in sight. On May 4, Elwood Wickerd reported that construction had begun on the last two miles of the road, which would bring the crews to Mile 22 from which the federal government would take over. It was estimated that construction would be completed by July 1, and then the prison camp could be removed from the mountains to Dripping Springs to work on reconstructing the road that led from the San Jacinto Valley to Warner's Hot Springs.[27] On May 11, the Board ordered the purchase of materials to begin the process of moving the camp to Dripping Springs.[28]

*Mile 23 - today's Cahuilla Tewanet vista point.
It is at this point that Riverside County's construction ended
and the federal government's began.*

On June 15, as work was winding down on the road, word came that an agreement had been reached between the Board of Supervisors and the federal government for construction of the road. In it, the Board agreed to construct one more mile of road, to Mile 23, which would give virtually all of the desert portion of the road's construction to federal officials. Therefore, removal of the prison camp was delayed to September 1 as Wickerd and his crews continued their efforts, now aimed at Mile 23.[29]

Throughout the summer of 1931, Wickerd and his crews continued construction of the last few miles of the highway, which traveled through the Pinyon Flats territory east toward Sugarloaf Mountain and Black Hill. The territory was very rocky at times and progress was slow. Finally, on September 5, 1931, the crews reached the Mile 23 point southeast of Black Hill and the last of the county's portion of the construction was completed.[30]

By September 5, 1930, construction of the Pines-to-Palms Highway had taken approximately 18 months over a two-year period, and cost the County of Riverside nearly $160,000.

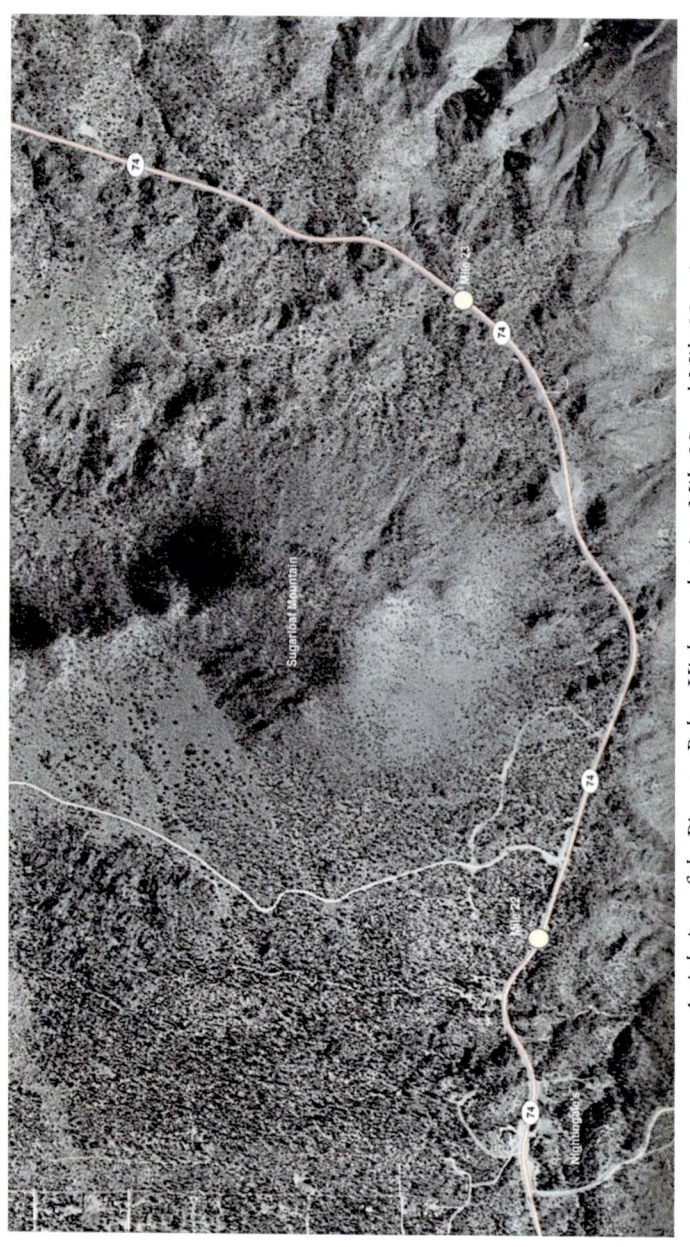

Aerial view of the Pines-to-Palms Highway showing Mile 22 and Mile 23 points

What the county had to show for its efforts was 23 miles of a compacted dirt/gravel road through some of the most spectacular scenery in the region. While the completion of the county's portion was not hailed in any great way, what was becoming obvious was that people were beginning to use the new road to explore the San Jacinto and Santa Rosa Mountains area and see for themselves many of the places they had only heard about in the newspapers or from friends. Now that the county was pulling out of the mountains and moving the prison road camp to Dripping Springs, anticipation began to build for the next phase of the project, which was to be undertaken by road contractors under contract with the federal government. The next ten miles, which would go through rocky slopes and very sandy areas, truly needed a more experienced hand in construction.

Pinyon Flats from the highway.
Mt. San Jacinto is in the distance to the left, Asbestos Mountain is to the right.

Chapter 4 Notes

1. San Jacinto Valley *Register*, August 15, 1929, Hemet *News*, August 16, 1929.

2. Hemet *News*, October 11, 1929.

3. That officials of Riverside County felt sure they could obtain rights-of-way while building the road is a testament to the times. It must be remembered that throughout the early history of Southern California, railroads, then later good automobile roads, that brought people into the area to settle and/or spend money were thought of as pieces of civic pride and a necessity to the livelihood of all towns. People in general gladly gave up part of their parcels for a railroad or street right-of-way, knowing that in all likelihood, it would bring an economic boon to the community, and of course raise their own property values. Sure, the Board authorized Wickerd's men to start on the road before the right-of-way was secured, but undoubtedly they had already had some talks with the landowners, and the landowners themselves could see the parade of survey stakes several months beforehand. Therefore, when it came time to actually obtaining the right-of-way from the Garners and the Lake Hemet Water Company, it was almost an assured deal.

4. Hemet *News*, January 17, 1930. Elwood Wickerd was praised for his running of the prison camp throughout the time that Riverside County built the Pines-to-Palms Highway. Noted for rampant corruption, prison road camps were generally looked down upon despite the fact that they were only a few years old at this point. Wickerd, however, ran a tight operation, managed to bring down the per-person cost of feeding and housing the inmates, and was noted for his ability to change the men under him while they were sentenced to his custody (Hemet *News*, March 7, 1930).

5. Hemet *News*, January 10, 1930.

6. Riverside County Board of Supervisor's minutes, March 3, 1930.

7. One item that Wickerd and his crews had to contend with was artesian water. Nearly everywhere they dug in the area, water was found. Wickerd even reported that in digging test holes for the bridges, two-foot streams of water would be sent into the air (Indio *Date Palm*, July 25, 1930).

8. Indio *Date Palm*, July 25, 1930.

9. This would be approximately 40 acres of land given a right-of-way 80 feet in width, assuming the Pinyon Flats route was chosen. No estimate was given for the Palm Canyon route right-of-way.

10. Hemet *News*, April 11, 1930.
11. No indication as to when these meetings were could be established. They were simply referred to in the past by later articles and references.
12. Riverside Daily *Press*, August 11, 1930.
13. Hemet *News*, August 29, 1930.
14. Hemet *News*, September 9, 1930. The county at this time was also negotiating with Robert Garner who agreed to pay for a portion of the 14 miles of fencing, together with cattle crossings and cattle guards, that would be needed along both sides of the highway to protect his cattle from automobiles and to protect motorists from cattle.
15. Indio *Date Palm*, September 19, 1930.
16. Indio *Date Palm*, September 19, 1930.
17. Indio *Date Palm*, September 19, 1930.
18. Indio *Date Palm*, October 10, 1930.
19. Indio *Date Palm*, October 10, 1930, Hemet *News*, October 10, 1930.
20. Riverside County Board of Supervisors' Minutes, October 20, 1930.
21. Indio *Date Palm*, October 24, 1930. During this era, federal regulations required that all interactions with Indians be handled through the Bureau of Indian Affairs. While local governments could enter into talks, no official business could be accomplished except through the Bureau. This is why the payment was made to the Bureau and not directly to the Santa Rosas. This method, needless to say, garnered much criticism here in Southern California. During the talks with the Santa Rosas for right-of-way, there were still talks going on with the Agua Caliente Band to obtain a right-of-way to Palm Canyon. The Riverside *Press* editorialized on April 28, 1931:

> The experience of the Santa Rosa Indians in having the $4000 which Riverside county appropriated for rights of way through their lands tied up in Washington by official red tape for several months, will certainly not make any easier the solution of the existing problems with the Palm Springs Indians regarding access to Palm canyon and the acquisition of the canyon as a national monument. We cannot blame these Indians much for wanting "cash down" before they part with any of their property. They could have that if they were dealing with Riverside county alone, but governmental regulations require all payments to be sent to Washington. Then the Indians are asked to wait indefinitely while the official red tape is unwound

that will enable them to get what belongs to them, if ever. The Santa Rosa situation has improved somewhat since earlier reports, but at the best it does not make one proud of the federal administration of Indian affairs.

22. Hemet *News*, December 12, 1930.
23. This had been considered for a number of months. The story of how the federal government entered into the building of the Pines-to-Palms Highway is related in Chapter 5.
24. Indio *Date Palm*, February 13, 1931.
25. Hemet *News*, February 27, 1931.
26. Hemet *News*, April 17, 1931.
27. Hemet *News*, May 8, 1931.
28. Riverside County Board of Supervisors' Minutes, May 11, 1931.
29. Hemet *News*, May 8 and June 26, 1931.
30. Hemet *News*, September 11, 1931.

Oak Grove across the highway from Vandeventer Flat

VIEW OF THE SEVEN SWITCHBACKS ON THE PALMS TO PINES HIGHWAY, CALIF.

Chapter 5
Construction by the Federal Government

To undertake the construction of a major road such as the Pines-to-Palms Highway was to be, Riverside County was stretching itself pretty thin in light of so many other projects and programs that were on the docket in the early years of the Great Depression. Although prison labor was available and being used to the greatest extent possible, it was becoming clear to those involved that using the work crews on the upper portion of the highway, where the terrain was flat and a road already existed, was one thing. Using these crews to carve a road out of the rocky hills of the desert with only one steam shovel available was quite another. If the road was to be completed in any sort of acceptable timeframe, help was going to have to be brought in from the outside. With these aspects in mind, coupled with the desire of both the state and federal governments to have greater access to the mountain area, it is no wonder that the Board of Supervisors began making overtures to the federal government for help. The federal government had already stepped in to construct a portion of the Hemet-Idyllwild road, so it was hoped, through negotiations with federal representatives, that they would also offer support for the new road to the desert.

Although mention of involving the federal government had been made for some time, it was not until after the route controversy was settled that overtures to the federal government were formally made. On November 3, 1930, Supervisor Thorndike Jameson addressed a letter to Charles Sweetser, the District Engineer with the Bureau of Public Roads, asking that the highway now under construction be adopted into the California Forest Highway System. This was a logical first step. Officials of the Forest Service seemed eager to help, and set a meeting with Supervisors Thorndike Jameson and William C. Moore, along with Alex Fulmor, Forest Service engineer Bruce B. Burnett, and Regional Engineer Edwin Kramer on Saturday November 15 to discuss the proposal.[1] There was one problem, though. Although most of the road being constructed fell within the boundaries of the National Forest, and was therefore eligible for inclusion in the Forest Highway System, the portion that the Supervisors were petitioning the federal government to construct was mostly outside the National Forest. The Forest Service stated that they were generally reluctant to spend federal monies outside of the National Forest. However, Stuart Show, the Regional Forester for the San Bernardino area, believed that the Pines-to-Palms Highway warranted special consideration:

> "Pines to Palms" road... seems to present unusual conditions which warrant special consideration and apparently justify making an exception in this particular case. Among the conditions I have in mind is the very fine work by your road crews and the considerable amount of County money already expended in constructing about fourteen miles of the project lying within the Forest Boundary. It is understood that you propose to continue construction

within the Forest to about mile 22 from where you suggest that Federal construction begin and extend to mile 32, a distance of 10 miles. From mile 32 to a connection with the paved County highway at mile 37.3, the construction will be undertaken by County forces.

While it is noted that about 8 miles of the 10 mile section you propose for Federal construction is outside the Forest boundary, it is noted also that his section apparently presents construction difficulties for which available county equipment and prison road crews are unsuited.[2]

Forester Stuart Show's reasoning rang true with his agency. On November 19, Show sent a letter to Charles Sweetser in San Francisco, this time recommending that the Pines-to-Palms Highway be included in the California Forest Highway System.[3] On Friday, November 21, the same Bureau of Public Roads, at another meeting with Jameson, Moore, Fulmor, Burnett and Kramer, agreed to set aside $150,000 in federal funds for the construction of the Pines-to-Palms road.[4] Whether the money would be used to construct a portion of the highway or to surface the entire road after the county crews finished was still to be determined. Most wanted the former, since, as Fulmor told the Board, "the working crew of the prison camp is necessarily limited by the number of inmates while a contractor to whom the federal contract might be let would be at freedom to employ as much help as he wished."[5] It was believed that the allotment by the Bureau of Public Roads, together with an accompanying federal contract to build about ten miles of the highway, would assure completion of the road by the spring of 1932.[6]

It was quickly decided that the federal government would continue construction of the road from the end of the county's portion to the connection with the Palm Springs-Indio Highway, at least initially. With this decision came authorization to use the initial allocation of funds, although inclusion of the road in the Federal Highway System was still being discussed. Therefore, the first action of the federal government toward construction of the Pines-to-Palms Highway was to send a highway engineer and a crew of surveyors to the site to familiarize themselves with the territory and review Fulmor's plans to determine if any improvements needed to be made. On December 14, Associate Highway Engineer James F. Waller arrived in Indio from San Francisco to begin the review of Fulmor's plans and to see for himself the task ahead. Waller soon assembled a crew of 15 to begin his field reconnaissance.[7]

On December 23, 1930, Secretary of Agriculture Arthur M. Hyde approved Show's recommendation to include the Pines-to-Palms Highway in the California Forest Highway system. This meant that the road's construction would be eligible for more highway money. Given that some estimates were running as high as approximately $400,000 for the highway's construction, the additional funding would be needed.[8] Throughout January of 1931, Waller's reconnaissance of the route continued while others tried to find and appropriate additional funds.

On February 9, 1931, James Waller's report of his field work and review of Fulmor's plans was made public to the Riverside County Board of Supervisors. Not only did Waller agree with most of Fulmor's plans, he truly believed that the proposed highway was a worthwhile endeavor:

> Riverside County has named this route the "Pines to Palms Highway." The name is very appropriate for in a distance of twenty miles one will be able to leave the palm trees in the desert at sea level elevation and be among the timber at an elevation of around 4500 feet. For this reason during the hot summer months, this road will have a great deal of traffic from the inhabitants of the desert, seeking a cool place to spend the nights. This road will also be

very attractive to tourists. The scenery differs from other scenery in California. The views of the desert, the views of Deep Canyon, and the distant view of Salton Sea will add greatly to the attractiveness of the road. This will also be a shorter route to the ocean than by the present roads from the desert. It is a worthy project and much needed by the residents of Coachella Valley.[9]

In his report, Waller indicated that the estimated cost to construct the highway from Mile 22 to Mile 37.3 (the connection with the Palm Springs-Indio Highway) would be $457,680.[10] This was broken down to approximately $293,000 for construction and the rest for surfacing and engineering. The only appropriation for construction at that time was $150,000, but it was mentioned that the Forest Service may appropriate an additional $150,000 for the project. While the Supervisors termed Waller's cost estimate "generous," there was little in it to cause concern and certainly not to stop the survey by federal engineers who were already at work below Black Hill in late February, 1931.[11] At the same time, Alex Fulmor told the Board that the federal survey would take at least until April 1 to complete. More good news came on March 6 when the Acting Secretary of Agriculture authorized a total of $250,000 for construction of the road, which was obviously closer to the construction estimates.[12]

The surveyors finished their final survey of the highway on March 23, 1931.[13] The road surveyed by the federal government was almost exactly the same as Fulmor's preliminary survey of several months before. A few changes were made on the descent of the ridge between Carrizo Canyon and Deep Canyon. In addition, there were to be two bridges spanning both Carrizo Creek and Dead Indian Creek.[14] The layout, though, was to be the same. The completed survey was sent to San Francisco, where construction managers were put to work formulating a request for bids to hire a contractor to actually complete the work. At the time, it was speculated that the work on the highway would commence sometime after July 1.[15]

As the federal government was working to begin construction on the lower portion of the highway, Road Superintendent Elwood Wickerd made a report to the Board of Supervisors on April 27, 1931, where he indicated that the crews were presently working in rough country at the Mile 19.5 mark with 2.5 miles to go for the county's portion of the road. A total of $168,000 had been expended to that date for all construction. More funds were needed to complete the county's portion since his fund had been almost exhausted. The Board appropriated an additional $5,000.[16]

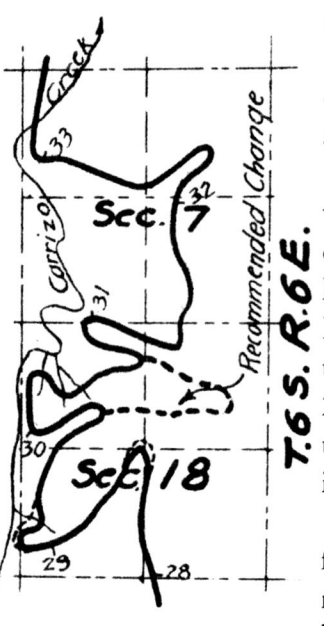

Waller's proposed changes to Fulmor's survey of the descent down Seven Level Hill (Photo courtesy National Archives)

Negotiations between the County of Riverside and the Bureau of Public Roads began in late April, 1931. A formal meeting was held on May 4 with all five Supervisors, Bruce Burnett (Assistant District Engineer for the U. S. Forest Service), Joseph Elliott (Forest Supervisor for the San Bernardino National Forest), and Alexander Fulmor. During the meeting, the Supervisors expressed their interest in having the federal officials begin construction at the Mile 32.5 mark near Dead Indian Creek and continue southwest into the mountains as far as funds would permit. A rough estimate made by the Bureau of Public Roads indicated that the allocation would run out at approximately Mile 24 (roughly one mile east of Sugarloaf Mountain), fully two miles east of the proposed end point of construction for Riverside County's portion. The Supervisors asked that if an additional $25,000 could be appropriated in federal funds, they would be willing to extend their construction point to Mile 23 (southeast side of Sugarloaf Mountain), where the two segments would meet. Burnett and Elliott seemed to believe that given the bidding climate at the time, they may be able to squeeze the additional mile out of bids that would probably be lower than those estimated.[17]

The Supervisors also asked if the bids for construction could be opened prior to July 1. For budgeting purposes, the Supervisors hoped to know how much money would be available for federal construction if bids came in lower than the estimates. While they expressed a willingness to construct the extra segment from Mile 22 to Mile 23, and the portion from the beginning of federal construction at Dead Indian Creek to the connection with the existing Palm Springs-Indio Highway (approximately four miles), they hoped that those two segments could be wrapped into the entire bid that the Bureau of Public Roads would be soliciting.

Burnett and Elliott proposed that the Bureau of Public Roads and Riverside County immediately enter into a cooperative agreement so that the request for bids could be issued at once, with bids potentially opening prior to July 1. However, none of that was to be. Reaching an agreement and finishing the plans and specifications would take a few months. In the end, the county signed the cooperative agreement on June 15, 1931, with the Secretary of Agriculture signing for the federal government on August 19, 1931.[18] By the time of the agreement, the Secretary of Agriculture had added an additional $75,000 in funds, bringing the total available to $325,000.

The plans, specifications, and engineering estimate for the roughly ten-mile stretch came to the Board on June 22. As presented, the federal government would build from Mile 23 to Mile 32.5 for an estimated $357,577, including two concrete bridges on the lower end. Due to the fact that there was only $325,000 budgeted for construction, it was estimated that the

$107,000 cost included for surfacing could be reduced, and, if need be, the $26,484 for the two bridges could be eliminated too.[19] The plans were found to be acceptable, and all parties hoped that the bids would come in below the estimated cost so that all of the proposed improvements could be made. At this point, though, all the authorities on both sides could do was to wait until the bids came in. It was hoped that they could be opened prior to the fiscal year end, but it took until the latter part of July for Forest Supervisor Joseph Elliot to even announce that bids would not be opened until August 11. At that time, it was estimated that the work would take about ten to twelve months to complete, and could be started as early as September 1.[20]

On August 11, three bids were received for construction of the ten-mile stretch. The low bid was submitted by the Yglesias Brothers of San Diego who bid $240,916.70.[21] Because the bid was well below the engineer's estimate, Joseph Elliott immediately forecast that the two bridges planned for Dead Indian Creek and Carrizo Creek could be built. While it was hoped that the remaining stretch of roadway connecting to the Palm Springs-Indio Highway could be built, it had been understood for a while that if there were funds left over, they would

The beginning of the road into the mountains
(Photo courtesy National Archives and Records Administration)

*Frank Cuffe, federal road contractor
(Photo courtesy Marshall Cuffe)*

be reappropriated to somewhere else.[22]

Construction began almost immediately after the agreement was signed on September 8. The Yglesias Brothers rented most of the 160 acre ranch of Raymond Wilson, located approximately ½ mile south of the Palm Springs-Indio Highway, for their headquarters.[23] A representative of the contractor indicated that he hoped to have the construction completed in 8-9 months. "May they have good luck and rush the job so that we can have some use of it during the hot weather next summer," a jubilant J. Win Wilson wrote.[24]

With the contract signed, the Yglesias Brothers, Santiago and Tomas, either sublet construction of the road to two subcontractors or abandoned it to them.[25] Frank Cuffe, a roadwork contractor from San Rafael, California and the second lowest bidder, was to begin where the county's construction efforts ended and work down toward the desert. Leo Honek, a Polish immigrant who owned an excavating contractor business in Los Angeles, was to start on the desert floor and work up to meet Cuffe and his crew somewhere along the way. Since the federal survey team had already staked the route and reviewed it several times, it was merely a matter of getting men and machines to the site, grading, blasting some areas, and smoothing to make the road fit the terrain.

At the same time that news was spreading of the Yglesias Brothers' mobilization on the project, it was announced that the county's portion of the road was complete. Prison camp superintendent Elwood Wickerd reported that the road crews had completed the last segment to Mile 23, and that the main prison road camp would be moved to Dripping Springs for use in constructing roads in the Aguanga area. The old prison camp would not be abandoned, though, but would continue to be occupied by juvenile offenders kept there to perform maintenance on the various mountain roads.[26] On October 2, the Hemet *News* reported that the men in the camp were finally being moved to Dripping Springs. In summing up the county's work on the Pines-to-Palms Highway, the *News* stated that:

Leo Honek and his wife Yetta
(Photo courtesy Milton and Mellow Honek)

> Twenty three miles southeast of Keen Camp, road crews of the county prison camp Saturday morning [September 26, 1931] completed the county's portion of the half million dollar Pines-to-Palms highway, scenic drive down the east slope of the San Jacinto and Santa Rosa mountains.
>
> Prison camp crews spent 18 months at work on the building of the initial 23 miles of the Pines-to-Palms highway. Not all of this time was used on that one project, however, as frequently they had to be called off for construction or repair of other places in the San Jacinto mountains. Several weeks work was put on the widening and re-aligning of the Hemet-Idyllwild road near the Idyllwild village.
>
> Another long delay was caused by the construction of the bridge over Herkey Creek, three

miles east of Keen Camp. The stone and concrete bridge required several weeks to complete and the steam shovel could not be moved across the creekbed until the bridge was finished.

Seven bridges were built along the course of the 23 miles, the longest, 180 feet in length.

Extending down the beautiful Hemet valley of the Kenworthy country, the first part of the road offered no great difficulty to the construction crews. Beyond Vandeventer flats, however, the right-of-way descends rapidly through a rocky terrain and construction slowed up tremendously at that stage of the work.

By mid-October, construction was progressing on both sides of the road segment under the federal road contract. Three steam shovels had been put to work, two on the northern portion and another on the southern portion in the mountains. "There is quite a city (tent city) at the Raymond Wilson ranch, where the contractors are encamped. . . The old road that was first broken by the Date Palm Pathfinder about four years ago, between the Indio-Palm Springs highway and the mouth of Dead Indian canyon, has been widened, leveled and very much improved by the contractors for their own convenience. It's

Steam shovel of Frank Cuffe at work on a road cut, 1932
(Photo courtesy Marshall Cuffe)

nice to drive up there now to see what is going on."[27] By the end of the month, a half-mile of roadway had been completed on the southern portion, the forms for the bridge over Dead Indian Creek had been set, and the two steam shovels were at work on what would become Seven Level Hill.[28]

The Wilson Ranch "city" mentioned above was the camp of Leo Honek and his crew. Each of the contractors established a separate camp where the employees stayed and ate while working on the project. One story to come out of this camp involved the Tune family. The construction company furnished lunch but no dinner, so the crews needed to go to either Indio or Palm Springs to arrange for that. The Tunes, Charlie and Ophelia, were working on the King Gillette grapefruit orchard on the main highway just west of where the Pines-to-Palms Highway would intersect. When Ophelia Tune heard of the need for a cook for an evening meal in camp, she offered to take on the responsibility and became the evening cook.[29] Charlie Tune, who was leery of his continued employment in the orchard, offered to work for Honek and became the dynamite handler – an important job that few people wanted.[30]

The other camp was located near the base of Sugarloaf Mountain and was operated by Arthur Nightingale and his wife Mae.[31] Nightingale had come to the Pinyon Flats area in 1928 or 1929 to subdivide land and sell lots in anticipation of the new highway, whichever route it was to take. When the federal engineers and surveyors came into the area, and later Frank Cuffe's crews, Nightingale began a camp of sorts and catered to them with meals. Nightingale's camp was located very near the Mile 22 mark on the road, since that was the initial stopping place for the county prison camp crews.[32]

Construction on the road continued throughout the fall of 1931 and the winter and spring of 1932. A few references to where the construction crews were at any given point were made in the papers of that time, but for the most part, progress on the road's construction seemed to be secondary to other news. Since the federal government's portion included only the section from the mouth of Dead Indian Canyon south,

Road graders at work at Deep Cut, 1932
(Photo courtesy Gary McKenzie)

the 4.15 mile stretch of road from there to the Palm Springs-Indio Highway still had to be improved. Straining the county budget, the Board authorized the Road Department to begin construction of that phase. Luckily, most of it had already been laid out and improved by J. Win Wilson several years before, and had been further improved as an access road for the contractors. This work was authorized in November, 1931.[33] Actual work did not start until late January, 1932.[34]

With construction progressing at three points, and the conclusion of the road in sight, the Board turned once again to the federal government to ask if there could be provisions for surfacing the new Pines-to-Palms Highway. Although it may seem strange to the modern reader, one must realize that during this time, constructing a highway of this type generally meant only grading and graveling the road. If funds permitted, the road could be surfaced with anything from a coating of road oil to macadam or even asphalt, but those types of treatments were not a given as they are today. As constructed, the Pines-to-Palms Highway was a compacted gravel road. Paving would come at a later date.

*Very early view of the Pines-to-Palms Highway showing gravel-only
road as originally constructed, circa 1932-1933
(Photo courtesy Historical Society of Palm Desert)*

The reason for wanting a surfacing treatment on the road was simply that the Board of Supervisors seemed to think that the road would see a lot of traffic once it was opened. Already, sightseers were using the section leaving Keen Camp to go observe the work being done by the federal contractors. The Board requested that the federal government treat the section from Keen Camp to Vandeventer Flats with an oil mix to set the gravel and ensure (hopefully) that the road would stand up to the anticipated traffic. Although many of the same players who fought to get federal funds for construction were in favor of the county's request, budgetary limitations made it impossible for the federal government to step in and fund any additional work on the highway at that time.[35]

Generally speaking, when people who were familiar with road building went to inspect the work being done on the last segment of the highway, most of them agreed that the work should be done around June, 1932. Heavy snowfall in February of that year halted construction for a few weeks. The situation was so bad at one point that people were worried about being able to get supplies to the work crews in the camps. The upper camp had been snowbound for a week and supplies had to be brought in by mule from the desert. The supply truck, it was reported, was lost in the snow somewhere between Keen Camp and the road camp.[36] By February, it was reported that crews on the upper portion were "a considerable distance this side of Black Hill and they have about a mile and a half of easy going ahead of them." Likewise, on the lower end, "progress . . . is good, although it appears to be slow. The heavy cuts and fills encountered are slow work, but the yardage made from day to day is quite satisfactory to all concerned."[37]

By mid-April, 1932, the two contractors were within sight of one another and an ironic situation was coming to pass. In reporting on the progress of the contractors, Riverside County Road Superintendent Rod McKenzie said the steam shovels working on both ends of the road were separated by a mere ten minute walk, but had about two months' work still to

View of construction on the Seven-Level Hill with both crews within sight of one another. Note trail just to the left of the car leadingbetween work sites, circa 1932 (Photo courtesy Marshall Cuffe)

complete. "High on the side of the mountain slope is the shovel of one crew and far below is the shovel of the second crew. . . A person can descend from the upper scene of operations to the lower crew in 10 minutes . . . but half an hour is required to ascend the slope." Work, however, was progressing well, and it was still reported that the road would be open for the summer season.[38]

In all, work on the road was going well, and people, especially those like J. Win Wilson who had been pushing the project for several years, could finally see the end in sight. Within a few months time, it would be possible to travel from Indio to the higher elevations in roughly 30 miles. The long struggle for the road, and the anticipation that its finishing brought, surely deserved a large-scale celebration – and that's exactly what was planned in the months ahead.

Chapter 5 Notes

1. Indio *Date Palm*, November 14, 1930, Show, Stuart B., Letter to Riverside County Supervisor T. C. Jameson, November 19, 1930 (National archives).

2. Show, Stuart B., Letter to Riverside County Supervisor T. C. Jameson, November 19, 1930 (National Archives). Mile 22 is on the southeast point of Sugarloaf Mountain, while mile 32 is about where the road comes out on the desert floor and begins its straight path to the Palm Springs-Indio Highway.

3. Show, Stuart, letter addressed only to "District Engineer, Bureau of Public Roads," November 19, 1930 (National Archives).

   ". . . it is believed desirable to include on the California Forest Highway System the entire project from the Idyllwild Forest Highway to a connection with the County paved road at Coachella Valley. We are also suggesting that an early survey be made of the ten mile section for which the County authorities request construction with Federal funds, and that your engineer check County plans of the remaining portion of the project in order to be assured that the standard conforms throughout."

4. The Riverside *Press* for November 10, 1930 had already indicated that the $150,000 may be allocated for the project.

5. Hemet *News*, November 14, 1930.

6. Hemet *News*, November 14, 1930.

7. Indio *Date Palm*, December 19, 1930.

8. Show, Stuart, letter to Board Chairman Thorndike Jameson, January 8, 1931 (National Archives), Hemet *News*, January 16, 1931, Indio *Date Palm*, January 16, 1931. Also at this time, the highway was designated as Highway 70 in the federal highway numbering system and named the Idyllwild-Desert National Forest Highway.

9. Waller, James F. "Reconnaissance Report – Idyllwild-Desert Forest Highway, Route No. 70, Riverside County, California." U. S. Department of Agriculture, Bureau of Public Roads, District #2 (n.d., although probably early February 1931).

10. *Ibid.* The costs were broken out as follows:

Total yardage of excavation	429,800 c. y.
429,800 c. y. at 60 cents	$257,880
Minor structures 10% of grading	25,790
Structures, Dead Indian Canyon	10,000
	$293,670
Crushed rock surfacing and oiling,	
15.3 miles at $8,000	122,400
Total	$416,070
10% Eng. & Conting.	41,610
Total estimated cost	$457,680

11. Hemet *News*, February 27, 1931. At this time, it was noted that the county's construction crews were at Mile 18 with just four miles to go before they would complete their segment.

12. Edwin Kramer, District Engineer, Bureau of Public Roads. Memo to Joseph E. Elliott, Forest Supervisor, San Bernardino Forest, March 11, 1931 (National Archives).

13. Indio *Date Palm*, March 27, 1931.

14. Indio *Date Palm*, April 3, 1931.

15. *Ibid.*

16. Hemet *News*, May 1, 1931, Riverside County Board of Supervisors' Minutes, April 27, 1931.

17. Hemet *News*, May 8, 1931. Show, Stuart B. Letter to Charles H. Sweetser (District Engineer, Bureau of Public Roads): May 12, 1931 (National Archives).

18. United States Department of Agriculture – Cooperative Agreement for the Construction and Maintenance of a National Forest Road (Idyllwild-Desert Forest Highway): August 19, 1931 (National Archives).

19. Indio *Date Palm*, June 26, 1931.

20. Indio *Date Palm*, July 24, 1931.

21. Indio *Date Palm*, August 14, 1931. The other two bids were by Frank Cuffe of San Rafael ($249,475.70) and Mathene S. Ross of

22. *Ibid.*

23. Indio *Date Palm*, September 11, 1931. The Wilson ranch was described as the southwest ¼ of Section 20, Township 5 South, Range 6 East (U. S. Bureau of Land Management, General Land Office Records – http://www.glorecords.blm.gov, accessed November 20, 2011).

24. Indio *Date Palm*, September 11, 1931.

25. Nothing official about this was announced in the newspapers or made available in the archives. What is known is that from this point on, the Yglesias Brothers firm is never mentioned again in reference to the Pines-to-Palms Highway. There is circumstantial evidence to indicate that this project was above the capabilities of the Yglesias Brothers, that they gave up trying to build the road from the desert, and sublet the whole contract to Cuffe and Honek. Regardless, Cuffe and Honek completed the Pines-to-Palms Highway, but there appears to be no formal contract with them and the federal government (various newspapers, NARA records, Quinn, December 15, 2011).

26. Hemet *News*, September 11, 1931. The prison road camp that had been used during construction of the Hemet-Idyllwild Road and then the Pines-to-Palms Highway is today known as McCall Memorial Park, located just north of Highway 74 about 1 mile west of the Highway 74/Highway 243 intersection. The road camp continued in use until it was abandoned in the 1950s. At that time, Supervisor Fred McCall asked that it be converted into an equestrian camp ground, which it was. Supervisor McCall died in office on December 25, 1963, and the next February, at the behest of several equestrian groups, the Riverside County Board of Supervisors officially changed the name of the park to McCall Memorial Park as it is known today (see Lech, *More Than a Place to Pitch a Tent*, pp. 113-118).

27. Indio *Date Palm*, October 16, 1931. The "Pathfinder" was J. Win Wilson's Model T Ford in which he and his family would take outings and then he would report back about his trip to his readers in the *Date Palm*. The road he's referring to is the one that he, Wilson Howell, and others graded and improved early in the campaign for a mountain-to-desert highway.

28. Indio *Date Palm*, October 30, 1931.

29. Likewise, when the crews needed their laundry done, Ophelia stepped in and became the laundress for the camp too.

30. Cavanaugh, Lucille (daughter of Charlie and Ophelia Tune), personal communication with the author, January 16, 2012. Although the King Gillette grove was profitable, Tune and several others saw that the soil of the area was quickly depleting and the grove would not last. Charlie Tune knew nothing about handling dynamite, but was willing to learn. Lucille Cavanaugh stated that handling the dynamite was a good-paying job, especially in the depths of the Great Depression.

31. Arthur Nightingale was born on October 16, 1896 in Minnesota. He was an experience mechanic and machinist, working in Oakland in 1920 as an auto mechanic and as a mechanical engineer in 1930 in Los Angeles (census and birth records per Ancestry.com). Nightingale's tenure at Pinyon Flats must have been intermittent until about 1931 when he needed to attend to the camp on a regular basis.

32. Quinn, Harry. Personal communication with the author, December 16, 2011. Harry Quinn knew Arthur Nightingale, who told him of his coming to the Pinyon Flats area.

33. Riverside Daily *Press*, November 23, 1931, Indio *Date Palm*, November 27, 1931.

34. Indio *Date Palm*, January 22, 1932. Stating that every resource was being strained to complete the Pines-to-Palms Highway segment on the desert floor, the Board grappled with how it would come up with the funds. One clever way they tried to use was to commandeer materials from illegal liquor operations for use in the camps. Construction of the road was occurring during the era of Prohibition, and although Riverside County had been a very dry county since its formation in 1893, its rural areas hosted many who did not necessarily share that temperance sentiment. Several months prior to March, 1932, a raid was conducted in Mira Loma wherein a boiler, steam pump and 127 sacks of sugar were seized by federal authorities who in turn gave the machinery to the prison camp and the sugar to the jail. Likewise, in a raid along the Beaumont-Redlands

View of the Coachella Valley from the Pines-to-Palms Highway, circa 1932
(Photo courtesy National Archives and Records Administration)

Highway, twelve 5,000-gallon vats were seized, four of which were given to the prison camp. However, federal authorities soon ended this practice when they determined that materials seized in raids on such operations could not be given to entities outside of the federal government (report of Joseph Elliott, San Bernardino Forest Supervisor, to the Riverside County Board of Supervisors, March 7, 1932, as reported in the Indio *Date Palm*, March 11, 1932).

35. Hemet *News*, December 28, 1931.
36. Indio *Date Palm*, February 19, 1932.
37. Indio *Date Palm*, February 12, 1932. According to Leo Honek's son Milton Honek, there were many problems encountered with the construction from the desert up the side of the hill. Several landslides in the loose dirt kept causing delays, and Leo Honek almost went broke on the job. Driving the segment today, one has little doubt that this could be true. There are several deep cuts in solid rock, and the sandy soil there is very loose, making it ripe for landslides (Honek, December 1, 2011).
38. Indio *Date Palm*, April 15, 1932.

Chapter 6
Opening the Road

As construction of the Pines-to-Palms Highway drew to a close, anticipation of its opening grew. Civic leaders, businessmen, members of various organizations, and the general motoring public began to prepare for what would prove to be a big event for the grand opening of the highway. The call for a large celebration was first heard during the summer of 1931 when bids for federal construction were opened and found to be low. Planning for the celebration, however, did not get underway until the spring of 1932.

In late April, 1932, it was announced that plans for a celebration were proceeding on two fronts. The San Jacinto Mountain Chamber of Commerce, centered in Idyllwild, was making preparations on the mountain end of the road, while J. Win Wilson was leading the committee centered around Indio and the Coachella Valley. Although preliminary plans were in the works, what remained a question was the actual date the road would be usable. It was hoped that the road could be open by June 1, but according to Alex Fulmor, it seemed as though June 15 would be a more likely date.[1]

Almost immediately upon announcement of the plans for a celebration, people began to come forward to help. J. Win Wilson addressed a letter to the Riverside County Board of Supervisors asking for official sanction of the celebration. The Board sent the letter to James Davis, the secretary of the Riverside County Chamber of Commerce, who in turn began making preparations for the official invitations. Robert and Anita Elliott, owners of the Tahquitz Lodge at Keen Camp, offered the use of their facility for the event, plus indicated they would provide the music, the dancing pavilion, and one whole steer for a barbeque.[2]

As plans progressed for the celebration, publicity for the new road also increased. Articles appeared in newspapers throughout Southern California, and other people who were involved talked about the new road at every chance they could get. It was noted that because of the heavy rain and snowfall of the previous winter, flowers were in bloom throughout the mountain territory and the desert, doubtless as an invitation to motorists to come see the area and drive the new highway.[3] One of the more embellishing articles about the highway itself came from the Los Angeles *Examiner*, whose reporter Seymour Rhodes could barely contain his enthusiasm:

> "Dominion over palm and pine." That was Rudyard Kipling's line in his "Recessional" to express the far-reaching spread of the British Empire.
>
> But here, in the empire which the Southern California motorist claims as his own, the phrase will soon carry no such broad meaning.
>
> A road in the making, the new "Palms-to-Pines" highway, which in the space of a little more than a dozen miles will carry the motorist from the floor of the Colorado desert, with its canyons filled with native palms, to the high slopes of magnificent San

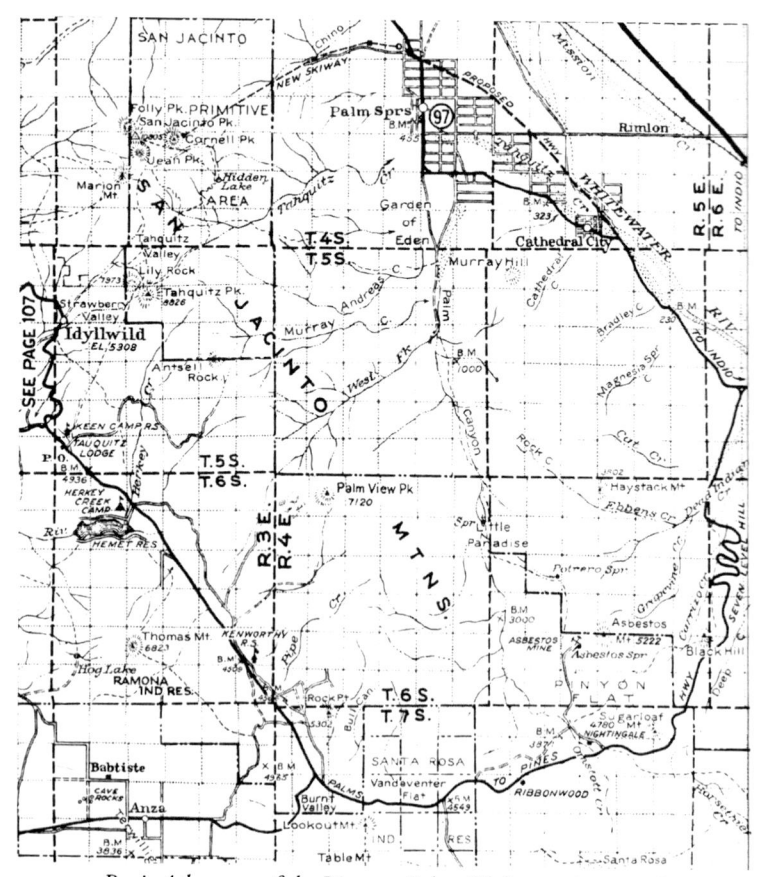

*Renie Atlas map of the Pines-to-Palms Highway, circa 1936.
Note locations of Tauquitz (sp) Lodge, Ribbonwood,
Nightingale, and the Seven Level Hill.*

Jacinto peak, studded thickly with pines, and in the winter months, deeply covered with snow.

It is a transition not to be found elsewhere in the world in such a brief distance, and this road, which early summer will see open to the motorist, is bound to take rank at once as a highway of the most dramatic contrasts to be found in America.

Its opening will mean that the motorist who loves both mountain and desert can combine the two in a one-day trip, circle San Jacinto peak, and climb from perhaps 200 feet above sea level to the mile-high resorts of Idyllwild and Keen Camp.

Work now is proceeding from both the upper and the lower ends, and present progress indicates that the road will be open and ready for travel by July 1.

Two big shovels, a fleet of trucks and all the paraphernalia of modern road building are at work on the lower end of the road. Between three and four miles is practically complete. The road climbs a ridge between Dead Indian canyon and Deep canyon that heads far back in mysterious Santa Rosa peak.

The upper end of the ten-mile section will emerge on Pinon Flat. Here, at the altitude of 4000 feet, the character of the country has changed materially. A fine stand of pinon pines and juniper bear witness to the heavier precipitation at these altitudes.

At Pinon Flat the road begins that already has been constructed by prison camp labor. It leads past the head of Palm canyon to Vandeventer Flat. Here, with startling suddenness, the reign of the desert ends. Great live oaks dot Vandeventer Flat, willows line Onstott Creek, and the gaunt red-shank makes a wall along the road.

Nowhere else can be seen a more sharply drawn line of demarcation between the desert and typical mountain forest growth. From this point all the way to Keen Camp the road traverses an almost level mountain mesa at an elevation of between four and five thousand feet, dotted here and there with pines that increase in number and beauty as the road approaches Keen Camp.

At Keen Camp the new road joins the present paved highway down the west slope of San Jacinto to Hemet. It will be only 68 miles from Indio to Hemet when the road is open, and of this distance 31 miles is already paved.[4]

Finally, June 18 was chosen as the date for the official opening ceremonies for the new highway. The formal announcement of the date was made at a meeting of the Riverside County Chamber of Commerce that was attended by California's Lieutenant Governor Frank F. Merriam.[5] Work on the road was rushed to be ready for the planned event. With only two weeks to go before the ceremony, though, J. Win Wilson and others went to Idyllwild for a final meeting regarding preparations. He and his group got as far as the place where the contractors were bogged down on a very large cut, and then had to walk across what he termed the "hole in the wall."[6] There, they were met by automobiles sent from Idyllwild to bring them to the meeting.[7] While at that meeting, the committee issued a program for the events of the day, which is reproduced as Appendix J.

For the next two weeks, the contractors labored furiously to try to get the road in shape for the opening ceremonies. By this time, most people were in agreement that the road would not be complete by then, and would probably take at least another month to actually finish construction. However, making the road passable was the main goal so that the planned activities could go ahead and people coming from all parts of Southern California could at least see the road in its near-completed state. The contractors succeeded, because by the

Frank Cuffe's construction crews working hard at the "hole in the wall," later known as Deep Cut, 1932. (Photo courtesy Marshall Cuffe)

weekend of June 18, the road was usable, but certainly not complete.

The events of Saturday June 18, 1932, began at 8:00 a.m. as cars from the Coachella Valley began to arrive at Deep Cut, where the contractors had met and where J. Win Wilson and his committee had decided to hold a ribbon-cutting ceremony to start the day. By 9:00 a.m., approximately 250 people had arrived and the ceremony could begin. The first people to be recognized were those who had helped J. Win Wilson and Wilson Howell perform some of the first work on the highway nearly four years before.[8] They included Charles Green, Billy Ford, Wilson Howell, J. Win Wilson and his wife Josephine, Arthur Wood and his wife Clara, Dr. Harry Smiley and his wife Nellie, Charles and Helena Wise, Charles Sinclair and his wife Charlotte, and Harry and Agnes Whittlesey.[9] Then, the federal engineers and many of the members of the contractors' construction crews stood across the road while the two contractors, Leo Honek and Frank Cuffe, stretched a silver in front of them. At the direction of J. Win Wilson, Mary Smith, a Girl Scout from Indio, and Charles Sanders, a Boy Scout from Coachella, cut the silver ribbon and "removed the last barrier that obstructed our way to the mountains."[10]

With the ribbon cut, the attendees got into their cars and leisurely drove up the new highway toward Keen Camp. Several stops were made along the way to examine the scenery, the vistas, or points of interest that were newly-opened by the highway. As noon approached, the party came to the Tahquitz Lodge at Keen Camp and joined a larger group that had assembled from Idyllwild, Hemet, Riverside, and throughout Southern California.

At noon, the crowd that had now grown to 1,100 in number enjoyed a large pit barbecue overseen by Harry Bergman of Aguanga. Bergman had barbecued two full steers, and others, including the A. M. Lewis grocery company of Riverside and Elmer Replogle (a merchant in Valle Vista) pitched in most of the rest of the feast, which included beans, pickles, coffee, and

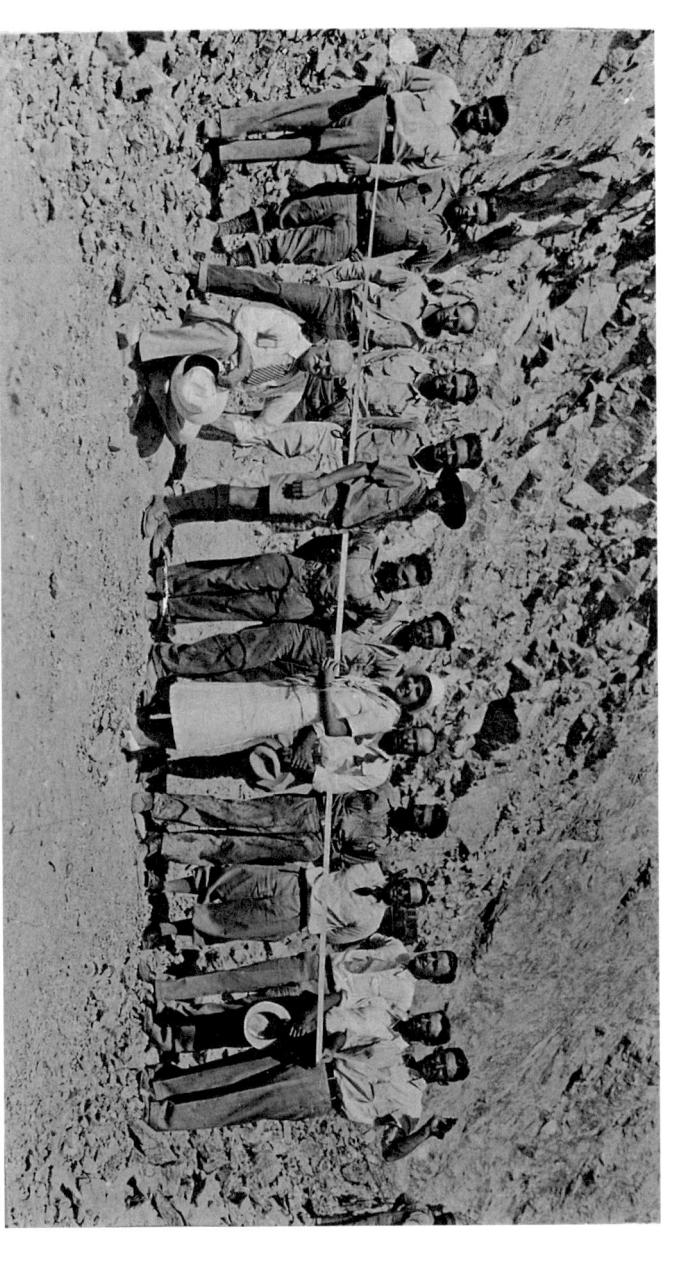

Before the ribbon cutting, June 18, 1932. Standing at far left is Leo Honek and at far right is Frank Caffe. Kneeling in front is J. Win Wilson, and next to him is Boy Scout Charles Sanders. The rest of the people are unidentified, but probably crew members of Honek's or Caffe's firms. (Photos courtesy Marshall Caffe)

bread. By 2:00 p.m., everyone had been fed and the main part of the program could begin. The master of ceremonies was Indio date farmer Bartlett Hayes who began by recognizing many of the dignitaries present, among whom where Los Angeles County Supervisor Hugh Thatcher, engineer John Applegate from the Bureau of Public Lands, engineer Ernest E. East from the Automobile Club of Southern California, and Riverside County Supervisors John Shaver, Robert Dillon, Thorndike Jameson, and Jack McGregor, who pleased the crowd greatly by calling on the entire San Jacinto mountain area to be closed to all hunting for posterity.[11] Hayes then gave a very inspirational dedication speech that detailed much of the history of the beginnings of the road while thanking the many people who either physically constructed the road or had a hand in its development. Chief among those, of course, were J. Win Wilson and Wilson Howell:

> I am one of those who always believes in bestowing honor and recognition on all those citizens who accomplish some outstanding act for the good of the community "outside the line of duty."
>
> Two men, Win Wilson and Wilson Howell, conceived the idea of this road and fostered it. To their everlasting credit let it be said that their every act and thought in the movement has been to advance the health and welfare of the people of Coachella valley.[12]

Among those who Hayes singled out for special recognition were the Santa Rosa Indians who, he said, "have granted us the right to pass through this Reservation, but let us not forget that we, one and all, must guard their property against trespass, against fire, against any other destructive act perpetrated through careless thought or otherwise. We salute these Indian friends and, with gratitude, the citizens of Coachella valley pledge them loyal support" (the full text of Hayes' speech at the dedication ceremony is reprinted as Appendix K).

The rest of the afternoon was spent in socializing and making trips along the road to see the sights. At 8:00 p.m. that evening, a dance was held in the pavilion of Tahquitz Lodge that was a big event. The next morning, for those who had decided to spend the night in the area, the pavilion was converted into a church and the Rev. Stanley Bond of the Christian Church of Coachella gave a sermon appropriately titled "The Highways to the Highlands of Life." Although the church services were well attended, the crowd was noticeably smaller than that of the day before.[13]

On Sunday June 19, the day after the official opening ceremony, the Riverside *Enterprise* summed up the pride that was undoubtedly felt by many who had worked so hard for the realization of the highway:

> "Good roads are the greatest of all improvements," wrote Adam Smith in his "Wealth of Nations." The great economist referred to the busy ways that traverse his native land. But there is no highway in the British Isles that compares in scenic splendor with Riverside county's Pines-to-Palms highway, which yesterday was formally declared open. And we question whether there is another road in all the United States that presents the diverse and contrasting scenic attractions this mountain-to-desert route offers.
>
> Starting a mile above sea level, where the sky seems near and where the air is fragrant with the balm of pine trees, this remarkable road descends the eastern slopes of the San Jacinto mountain range. Winding through the green and cool mountain valleys, it takes its way downward to the tawny, arid vastness of the desert. Emerging from a canyon, between groves of tropic palm trees, it terminates below the level of the sea.

In the Pines-to-Palms highway Riverside county has a scenic route that can rank with the worlds famous roads.

But the highway also has its utilitarian phase. It offers residents of the Coachella valley a shorter, more rapid means of entrance and exit to the San Jacinto mountain resorts.

The construction of the Pines-to-Palms highway constitutes an engineering achievement of note. It was built through a wilderness that offered hindrances of a difficult nature. That it has only easy gradings and a minimum of curves is a fine testimonial to the engineers who laid it out. Its construction has been accomplished expeditiously and at a very low cost.

Twenty-three miles were built by the county prison crews under the direction of Supt. E. C. Wickerd. This portion of the highway extends from Keen Camp 23 miles eastward ending near Sugarloaf hill, adjoining Pinon Flats. The next 10 miles, between the end of the prison camp road and the point where the right-of-way drops down out of the hills to the desert in Indian canyon, were constructed by two or three firms under a $350,000 Federal contract. The connecting link between the end of the Federal work and the Palm Springs-Indio highway was built and oiled by Supt. R. L. McKenzie's county highway department.

The Pines-to-Palms highway is a project of which Riverside county citizens justly can be proud. It should prove a valuable asset to the county.

As is typical of events that are planned months in advance, the opening ceremony was held before the road itself had been completed. During the days leading up to the ceremony, the contractors worked furiously to ensure that the one last portion was at least passable, but starting Monday June 20, work resumed on the final link with travel being allowed only at certain hours. However, so many people, enthusiastic to drive the new route, came through and demanded access at all hours, that within the first week, the contractors had to announce that all access to the route would be prohibited until at least July 3.[14]

On Sunday, July 3, a few people ventured along the highway and found it open, so took advantage of it. However, periodic closings continued. A week later, on July 11, the Riverside County Board of Supervisors received word from Charles Sweetser in San Francisco that the contractors should have the work completed no later than Friday, July 15. It wasn't until the weekend of July 23-24, though, than any official proclamation was made stating emphatically that the road would not only be open for travel, but free from further closings. On those two days, the road was heavily traveled. "The information that the Pinon Pines road was open for travel very quickly spread around the valley last weekend and the result was a good crowd in the mountains for the Sunday outing. . . . According to the speedometer . . . it is 27 miles from Indio to Nightingale's camp; 43 miles to Herkey creek, and 47 miles to Keen Camp. The day was delightfully cool and refreshing and everyone appeared to enjoy the outing to the limit."[15]

With construction work completed, the highway was opened and became an immediate success. Thousands of motorists flocked to see the new highway and drive from the mountains to the desert, all in their own cars. Residents of the Coachella Valley, eager to escape the heat, flocked to the higher elevations and camped, rented cabins, or bought property in the Pinyon Flats area upon which they would soon build cabins. One year later, the Riverside *Press* acknowledged that:

> Besides having become a widely-famed link in a scenic loop drive from Los Angeles to Palm Springs and return, the Pines-to-Palms

Highway this summer has carried heavy travel of Coachella Valley residents who escape the blistering night heat of the low valley by driving to the cool mountain heights.

Several subdivisions have been established in the vicinity of Pinon Flats and westward to the country of the Santa Rosa Indian reservation. Mountain cabins are rising rapidly throughout the country at the base of Thomas mountain of the Santa Rosa mountain range which the scenic highway skirts.[16]

In fact, so many people used the highway in the months after the contract work was completed that the road soon began showing signs of wear. Work on the highway was still needed in the view of several people. In July, the Board of Supervisors asked the federal government to oil the highway as a method of surfacing treatment. That request was declined, but later in the summer, it was announced that the U. S. Forest Service would put down a two-inch gravel treatment on the 17 miles extending east from Keen Camp. This would treat the road between Keen Camp and the bridge over Palm Canyon at Vandeventer Flats and was part of was what termed "emergency relief legislation" that was passed by Congress in the early days of the Franklin Roosevelt administration.[17] The material, approximately 200,000 cubic yards, would be mined from along the route.[18]

Surfacing of the highway with crushed rock helped the situation, but due to ever-increasing traffic, it was determined that a more stable solution would be needed. In July 1933, it was announced that a new contract for surfacing, this time with a more permanent oil mixture, had been approved through the Forest Service and the Riverside County Board of Supervisors.[19] Because bids for the original contract to simply gravel the surface had come in well below the estimated cost, it was hoped that the entire length of the highway to Mile

*Oiling the Pines-to-Palms Highway, 1933
(Photo courtesy National Archives and Records Administration)*

33 could be treated. Under this contract, the county would mix and spread the oiled gravel with the federal government purchasing the material and providing the machinery. August 3 would be the date for bids to be opened, with approximately two to three months needed for the work itself.[20]

Unfortunately for Superintendent Rod McKenzie, who was already at work preparing the roadbed to receive the oil mix, the bid documents were mislaid and a delay of several days occurred. When it was finally awarded, Clyde W. Wood of Stockton was found to be the low bidder, delivering 780,000 gallons of road oil to the project site for $31,000, or just under 4¢ per gallon.[21] Work began on August 23, 1933 and was rushed to ensure the mountain portion of the surfacing could be completed before cooler weather set in. The mountain portion was finished around October 1, and the crews were moved to the desert side, where they finished treating the road around the 9th of November.[22] True to form, J. Win Wilson hosted a picnic at Pinyon Flats on November 12 to celebrate the surfacing of the road, which could now better handle the throngs of people who were "discovering" the new mountain-to-desert road.

A crowd stops to admire the view of the Coachella Valley along the newly-oiled Pines-to-Palms Highway, circa 1936 (Photo courtesy National Archives and Records Administration)

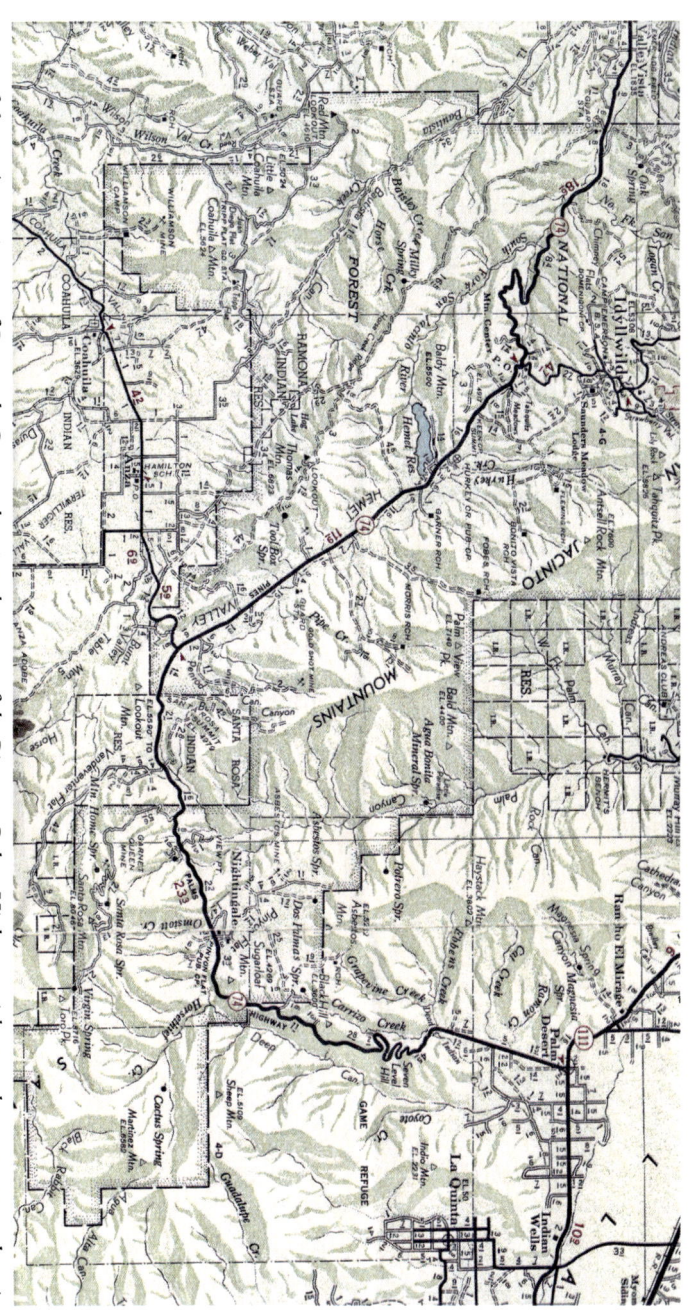

Portion of the 1948 AAA map of Riverside County showing the route of the Pines-to-Palms Highway with several contemporary locations. (Photo courtesy Automobile Club of Southern California)

The Ensuing Years

The opening of the Pines-to-Palms Highway in July, 1932, and the improvements made to it over the next year, were a tourism boon for Riverside County. Over the next several months and years, tours of the highway, geared toward newspapermen and elected officials and sponsored by J. Win Wilson, brought hundreds of people to the area, most of whom returned to their respective cities and wrote about the wonders of the highway in their newspapers, or touted them to church meetings, club gatherings, and just word-of-mouth (one such article, from the Los Angeles *Times*, entitled "New Highway Over San Jacinto Mountain Area," is reproduced as Appendix L). This advertising in turn sent many thousands of people to the area to see for themselves the wonder of the new road.

Continued upgrades to the road meant that those who used it could do so more comfortably than before. In 1937, the highway was paved and put under the auspices of the State of California, as it still is today. Sometime during this era, a water stop was installed on the sharp curve just below Vista Point. It consisted of a rock and concrete column with a drinking fountain on the top and a faucet on the side. This would allow motorists to fill their car's radiator after the uphill climb from the desert. Rock work, which can be seen on the desert side of the road, was completed by William Bradford and Jack Snow, both of Anza.[23] This rock work is very indicative of the type of work that is along all three of the routes between the San Jacinto Mountains and the valleys below.

One of the largest improvements to occur along the scenic highway happened in the post-war years as brothers Randall, Phil, Carl and Cliff Henderson, together with their brother-in-law Tommy Tomson, developed the town, and later city, of Palm Desert at the desert end of the Pines-to-Palms Highway. These men, together with investors Leonard Firestone, Harold Lloyd, and Edgar Bergen, developed the Shadow Mountain Club and subdivided their 1,600 acres of land into the townsite that today is one of the major cities within the Coachella Valley.

By the 1960s, the State of California was developing criteria to designate certain highways within the State as Scenic Highways. In 1963, the California Legislature adopted a master plan for State Scenic Highways. Among those listed was the Pines-to-Palms Highway, which was said to have "the outstanding qualities to qualify as a State Scenic Highway."[24] In 1969, Riverside County developed a proposal under the state guidelines to designate all three of the routes into the San Jacinto Mountains as Scenic Highways. The proposal outlined several items that should be maintained in order to assure the Pines-to-Palms Highway remain a scenic highway for everyone to enjoy.[25] The designation was accepted, and since October 18, 1971, the highway has been a State Scenic Highway.

Today, the highway has been further upgraded to make it more conducive to the faster speeds drivers use today. Because most modern vehicle trips are made with a purpose other than the sheer pleasure of driving, fewer drivers take the time to stop and appreciate the unique setting that is the Pines-to-Palms Highway. Fewer still probably even know about the civic-mindedness and community pride that went into the lobbying for and construction of the highway. It is the author's hope that this book will help in some small way to change that.

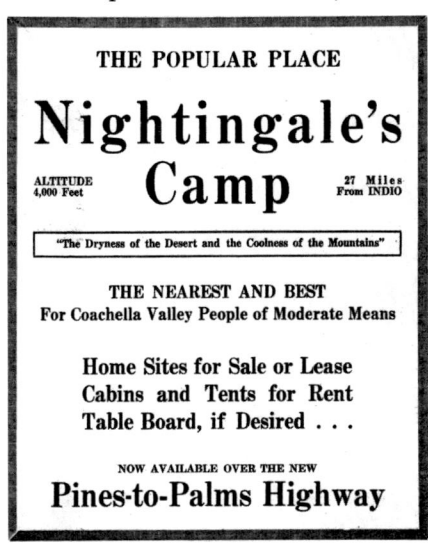

```
THE POPULAR PLACE
Nightingale's
ALTITUDE                          27 Miles
4,000 Feet       Camp             From INDIO

"The Dryness of the Desert and the Coolness of the Mountains"

THE NEAREST AND BEST
For Coachella Valley People of Moderate Means

Home Sites for Sale or Lease
Cabins and Tents for Rent
Table Board, if Desired . . .

NOW AVAILABLE OVER THE NEW
Pines-to-Palms Highway
```

(Top) Deep Cut today
(Bottom) Roderick McKenzie's Riverside County
road crew, circa early 1930s
(Bottom photo courtesy Gary McKenzie)

Chapter 6 Notes

1. Hemet *News*, May 6, 1932.
2. Indio *Date Palm*, May 13, 1932.
3. Indio *Date Palm*, June 3, 1932.
4. Los Angeles *Examiner*, March 20, 1932.
5. Indio *Date Palm*, May 27, 1932. This meeting was held in International Park (now Bogart Park) in Cherry Valley. The County Chamber pledged $200 toward the festivities.
6. This "hole in the wall" was almost literally correct. The place where the contractors met was to be called "Deep Cut" and is a particularly deep cut in the rock going around a curve in the road. It would become a landmark for years, and has of late gotten the moniker "Dead Man's Curve."
7. Indio *Date Palm*, June 10, 1932. One can only imagine how forcefully Wilson made his case to the contractors that the road must be open by June 18!
8. This work was the grubbing and dragging of the road from the Palm Springs-Indio highway south to where Dead Indian Creek came out of the mountains.
9. All of these listed people were from Indio. Charles Green was a hotel proprietor, Billy Ford was the 18-year-old son of a locomotive engineer, Arthur Wood was the proprictor of a service station in Indio (his wife was Clara), Dr. Harry Smiley was a general practice physician (his wife was Nellie), Charles Wise was a mule and horse dealer and his wife Helena an artist, Charles Sinclair was a house carpenter (his wife was Charlotte), and Harry Whittlesey was a farm manager (his wife was Agnes). Indio *Date Palm*, June 24, 1932, 1930 Federal Census Records, accessed from Ancestry.com.
10. Indio *Date Palm*, June 24, 1932.
11. Indio *Date Palm*, June 24, 1932, Riverside *Press*, June 18, 1932.
12. Hayes, Bartlett H., comments at the dedication of the Pines-to-Palms Highway, June 18, 1932, as reprinted in the Indio *Date Palm*, June 24, 1932.
13. Indio *Date Palm*, June 24, 1932.
14. Indio *Date Palm*, June 24, 1932.
15. Indio *Date Palm*, July 29, 1932. See page 126 for a discussion of Nightingale's Camp.

16. Riverside *Press*, July 25, 1933.
17. Riverside *Press*, August 8, 1932, Indio *Date Palm*, August 12, 1932.
18. Riverside *Press*, October 3, 1932.
19. Riverside *Press*, July 4, 1933.
20. Riverside *Press*, July 25, 1933.
21. Riverside *Press*, August 22, 1933.
22. Riverside *Press*, October 9 and November 6, 1933.
23. Quinn, Harry. Personal communication with the author, February 17 and 18, 2012.
24. Riverside County Planning Department, December, 1969, p. 2.
25. Among the criteria mentioned in the report are:
    a. Public utilities should be placed underground wherever possible.
    b. Restrictions on outdoor advertising should be maintained.
    c. The replacement and preservation of natural native plants should be encouraged.
    d. Scenic vistas, roadside rests, and picnic areas should be maintained and provided. Existing scenic vista points . . . should be maintained.
    e. An on-going citizens protective council charged with the prime responsibility of corridor protection should be established.
    f. Architectural and landscape controls should be improved and enforced.
    g. Urbanization should be directed toward community clusters through a land exchange program between private land owners and the federal government.
    h. In all cases, development should be compatible with scenic protection.
    i. The rights and conveniences of private land owners within the scenic corridor are to be safeguarded. (Riverside County Planning Department, December, 1969, pp. 26-27).

It's Cool at Mile-High
Idyllwild
Right at the Desert's Door

Plan now to spend your vacation or your week-ends at this popular San Jacinto mountain resort. The new

PINES-TO-PALMS

highway (open about June 1) brings Southern California's finest vacation land within a few hours drive of your home. Turn off Imperial Valley highway at Indio.

Idyllwild Offers You—

Hotel and housekeeping accommodations at new low rates—the finest mountain golf course in California—swimming—fishing—tennis—horseback riding—cool days and cooler nights.

MAKE RESERVATIONS NOW
Write Idyllwild Inn, Idyllwild, Calif.
CABIN SITES FOR SALE   10-13

Appendix A

Sites Along the Pines-to-Palms Highway

For those who may need to familiarize themselves with the geographic nomenclature of the area, the following list and description of place names is offered. These names were in use at the time of the highway's construction, and hence are used throughout the book. Some names have been replaced with others, and those are listed within the relevant place's discussion.

A. **Keen Camp** - This facility had been operated principally by Mary Keen as early as the 1890s. Keen Camp was a summer getaway, with regular conveyance service from the town of Florida (present-day Valle Vista just east of Hemet), where Mary's husband John operated the hotel there. Keen Camp became very well known, and by 1909 it was a recognized place name, complete with its own post office. In the 1920s, Keen Camp became the Tahquitz Lodge, a mountain resort run by Robert and Anita Elliott. Tahquitz Lodge was the scene of the dedication ceremony for the Pines-to-Palms Highway. In 1946, the name Keen Camp was abandoned when the post office was moved to the northwest to the interchange of Highways 243 and 74, and the name changed to Mountain Center.

Keen Camp, 1910s

B. **Herkey (Hurkey) Creek** – Herkey Creek is a tributary of Lake Hemet, extending into the mountains northeast of the lake. The name is variously spelled Herke – Herkey – or Hurkey, depending on the time. Regardless, the creek is named for a man about whom all is known is that his name was Mr. Herke. Herke was a wood cutter hired by the Thomas Ranch. One day, while out in the forest, Herke's dog treed a couple of bear cubs, much to the consternation of the mother bear. She took her frustration out on Herke, who managed to return to the ranch house despite his wounds. He succumbed to his wounds a few days later and was buried along the creek that bears his name. Herkey Creek was the first obstacle in building the Pines-to-Palms Highway. The public campground at Herkey Creek was begun only a few years earlier (for more on the Hurkcy Creek Park, as it is known today, see Lech, 2011, pp. 47-53).

Herkey Creek

C. **Lake Hemet** - Lake Hemet was formed in 1895 when the Hemet Dam was finished after several years of construction. The purpose of Lake Hemet was to provide irrigation and domestic water for the new town of Hemet to the west. With the advent of the Pines-to-Palms Highway, Lake Hemet was opened for recreational uses and remains a major landmark on the upper reaches of the highway.

Lake Hemet

D. **Hemet Valley** - The Hemet Valley is the large, flat mountain valley that generally stretches for several miles south of Herkey Creek. It has also been known as the Thomas Valley, and today is known as Garner Valley. The Hemet Valley is not to be confused with the valley in which the towns of Hemet and San Jacinto lie - that is the San Jacinto Valley. Regardless, the Hemet Valley saw much activity in the early 1890s with the construction of the Hemet Dam and the formation of Lake Hemet.

Horses grazing in the Garner Valley, 1930s

E. **Garner Valley** - The Hemet Valley has been known as Garner Valley since the early 1900s. It was named for owner Robert Garner. Previously, it was known as the Thomas Valley for Charles Thomas, who homesteaded and purchased land in the area starting as early as the 1870s. The Pines-to-Palms Highway stretches throughout the Garner Valley in the northern reaches.

F. **Vandeventer Flats** - This small meadow area was named for Frank Vandeventer, who had been a jack-of-all-trades during the early years, running a stage station in the desert before heading into the mountains in the 1870s. He settled at the area that would become Vandeventer Flats, which was at a crossroads in the mountains. From Vandeventer Flats, trails radiated out in all directions - to and down Palm Canyon, the lower Coachella Valley, Garner Valley, and west to the Cahuilla Valley. Vandeventer Flats played a key part in travel through the mountain area, and in turn would be a key location along the Pines-to-Palms Highway. Today it is the site of the Santa Rosa Indian Reservation.

Vandeventer Flats with Santa Rosa Mountain in the background

G. **Ribbonwood** – Between Vandeventer Flats and Pinyon Flats was a small stop on the road established by Wilson Howell. Here, Howell developed his desire for organic agriculture, constructed a brush ramada that served as a stopping point where motorists could get a drink or a hand-made trinket, and established a few rustic rental cabins. Howell's fascinating story, summed up in a previously-published article by the author, is reprinted as Appendix M.

H. **Pinyon Flats** - Heading east from Vandeventer Flats, one comes into Pinyon Flats, a much larger area and named for the dense Pinyon forests that once characterized the region. The Pinyon Pine was a vital part of the local Indians' subsistence pattern, and they would come to the area to collect Pinyon nuts, which like acorns and mesquite beans, were stored and eaten throughout the year.

I. **Asbestos Mountain** - Located north-northeast of Pinyon Flats, Asbestos Mountain is named for the asbestos deposits there that were mined for many years starting in the 1890s. At a time when making materials fireproof was an utmost concern (and certainly before the toxic properties of asbestos were known), asbestos mines were established in many places, with the mineral being highly prized for use in flooring, roofing, and other applications where fireproofing was warranted.

Asbestos Mountain

J. **Onstott Creek** - Sometimes referred to as Omstott Creek, this creek is one of many tributaries to Palm Canyon from the base of Santa Rosa Mountain. It is named for mountain hermit Myron M. Onstott. Onstott settled along the creek early in the history of the area and engaged in farming and cattle raising. He was well-known and well-liked, and helped all passersby who needed it. According to his obituary in the Los Angeles *Times* on February 13, 1908, he was well-educated and quite the conversationalist - but no one could figure out why he lived as a hermit.

K. **Deep Canyon** - The naming of this canyon is pretty obvious. As one travels down the Pines-to-Palms Highway into the desert, Deep Canyon lies to the east. It's deep gorge and precipitous walls make its moniker aptly applied.

Deep Canyon

(NOTE - Deep Canyon is now the Philip L. Boyd Deep Canyon Desert Research Center, a research field station of the University of California, Riverside and the University's Natural Reserve System. Public access to the site is restricted. The author was granted permission to photograph the site for this work, and is very grateful for that opportunity).

L.   **Sugarloaf Mountain** – So named because it is shaped like a sugarloaf, i.e. very conical and fairly symmetrical. Sugarloaf Mountain is at the very east end of Pinyon Flats and marks the transition between Pinyon Flats and the true desert side of the highway.

Sugarloaf Mountain

M. Dos Palmas Spring – This spring is located between Sugarloaf Mountain and Black Hill, and is the headwaters of Carrizo Creek. It was probably named around 1900 for the fact that two palms were seen growing there, Dos Palmas being the Spanish term for two palms. It was a noted watering hole along the trail that preceded the Pines-to-Palms Highway, and was mentioned as a place for water for automobiles if needed.

Dos Palmas Spring

N. Black Hill – A smallish hill facing Deep Canyon near the very top of the Seven-Level Hill. Black Hill is named because of its dark color. While Black Hill is rather a bit darker than the surrounding light, mineral-rich, soil, calling it black is a bit of a stretch. However, no other reason for calling it Black Hill could be ascertained – it was called that in contemporary citations, so the name has been around since at least the mid-1920s.

Black Hill

O. **Dead Indian Canyon/Creek** – According to J. Win Wilson, the naming of this creek and canyon came about from a story told to the white settlers by the native Cahuilla. Apparently several of their people were en route to Temecula for a conference with other Indian groups. One of the members died in the canyon, and was buried there, hence the name. Dead Indian Canyon and Creek were probably named in the 1890s. It should be pointed out that what constituted the canyon and creek in the 1920s and 1930s is slightly different than today. Today, it is simply the small canyon that lies due west of the levee across from the Santa Rosa/San Jacinto Mountains National Monument Visitor's Center. In the 1920s and 1930s, the name included all of that canyon plus all of the wash that extends from the canyon toward the highway.

Dead Indian Canyon

P. **Palm Canyon** - Another simple, descriptive name. Palm Canyon is named for the myriad of palms that line the bottom of it. The canyon is a major geographic feature of the eastern San Jacinto Mountain area, and as such played a vital role in travel from the desert to the mountains for thousands of years. Its steady incline starts just south of present-day Palm Springs and leads 15 miles up to the base of Santa Rosa Mountain. Palm Canyon was and still is a major tourist place for travel, hiking, study, and relaxation.

PALM CANYON NATIONAL MONUMENT, PALM SPRINGS, CALIFORNIA

Q. **Hermit's Bench/Haven** - The Hermit's Bench is known today as the location of the gift store at Palm Canyon. For many years beforehand, it was the home of William Pester, one of the colorful early residents of Palm Springs. Pester led a hermit's existence in Palm Canyon, eating natural foods, wearing very little clothing, and in general eschewing society at a time when that was a rarity (in fact, some sources refer to Pester as California's original hippie). Pester supplemented his income by taking odd jobs and allowing his photo to be taken by tourists for a little money. Eventually, his odd behavior got him forced out of the area, but the Hermit's Bench (or Hermit's Haven as it was sometimes called), is still listed on the maps today.

William Pester at his hermit's home in Palm Canyon

R. **Carrizo Canyon/Creek** – Carrizo Canyon, and the Creek that runs through it, are located between Deep Canyon and Dead Indian Canyon in the desert portion of the highway. Named for the Spanish word for the ubiquitous reed grass that grows throughout Southern California in wet, marshy areas, Carrizo Canyon was the location of the main trail leading from the desert to Dos Palmas and Pinyon Flats for the many years before the advent of the Pines-to-Palms Highway.

Carrizo Canyon

S. **Seven Level Hill** – This is a term given to the hill between Deep Canyon and Carrizo Canyon. Prior to the Pines-to-Palms Highway, it was unnamed, and simply referred to as the hill or ridge between Deep Canyon and Carrizo Canyon. When the highway was being constructed and it was necessary to carve a series of switchbacks into the side of the hill, the hill gained that name for the seven levels the road meanders along as it ascends from the desert floor to Pinyon Flats.

Seven-Level Hill with Coachella Valley in background, 1960s

Appendix B

From Pines to Palms

(Excerpted from George Wharton James' The Wonders of the Colorado Desert, *Chapter XXXIII, pp. 463-472)*

PIROUETTING like so many clowns and acrobats are the sparks that shoot out from our camp-fire. The flames dance and circle merrily and the burning mesquite wood crackles lustily. It is a beautiful evening in February and we are camped near the old town of San Jacinto on the west side of the great range of that name, the other sides of which gaze directly down upon the desert. The morning of the start is clear, bracing, and inspiring, and it seems a short tramp past the home of Mrs. Jordan, the Aunt Ri of "Ramona," to Florida and thence up the steep grades of the mountain to the pines.

But evening overtakes us. We make camp under the long-spreading branches of a big-cone spruce (*Pseudotsuga macrocarpa*). All around us is a dense growth of chaparral, the main feature of which is chamisal (*Adenostema fasciculatum*), with several species of manzanita (*Arctostaphylos*), ceanothus, mountain-mahogany (*Cercocarpus betulafolius*), and tree-poppy (*Dendromecon rigidum*) scattered throughout the mass. It is early and we determine to have a luxurious bed, so we gather a large pile of spruce branches and make a mattress of them on which we spread our blankets. Then in this sweetly odoriferous and soothing atmosphere, lulled by the wooing winds which kiss the pines and make them sing, we sink into a sleep, dreamless and reposeful, that few city dwellers ever enjoy.

In the morning it is hard work not to spend all the time in botanizing. The spring flowers are coming up in unusual profusion. Yonder is the big-root (*Echinocystis macrocarpa*), and as only one of us is familiar with the plant and the reason for its name, we stop long enough to dig it up. It is one of the most wonderful water-storage plants of the mountains, being to the higher regions what the barrel-cactus is to the desert. Its root is made for water storage, and we find that the specimen we have dug is gorged for a long, dry summer. It is as large around as a man's body and full of water.

Soon we pass a lumber camp, one of those relentless slaughter-houses of trees that have taken years to grow, and that ruthlessly denude the mountain slopes of their rich clothing of pines, firs, and spruces. We recognize the need of lumber, but we are bitterly opposed to the present methods of cutting it which take no thought for the morrow, stripping vast areas and never planting a seed for the future.

Allan's Camp, a picturesque summer resort, now seems desolate and forlorn. Its tents are all dismantled, but when the warmer days come the merry crowd of campers will come also, and then the woods will resound with happy voices, exuberant laughter, and the songs of men and women to whom the mountains have given new life, health, and strength.

Now we are fairly in the Hemet or Thomas Valley, the former name being given because on our right is the great Hemet Lake, caused by the Hemet Dam, and which supplies the town and vicinity of Hemet with water, and the latter name being that of our old friend Thomas, after whom the mountain yonder is named and to whose hospitable ranch-house our willing foot-steps are fast hastening us.

What a difference it makes when one is tired and hungry to feel that there is a glad welcome awaiting him ahead, where willing hands will minister to his comfort and cheerful voices and happy smiles make him feel at home! This is the Thomas habit. Many a traveler can tell of the warm-hearted hospitality of this whole family, from father to youngest son, from mother to youngest daughter.

As soon as we appear kind words greet us and we are bidden to enter with the courtesy of New England combined with the hearty and spontaneous welcome of California. Mr. Thomas left the East when a young man, sailing for the land of gold in the early days of the excitement. Soon he drifted from San Francisco to Santa Barbara, where he met his fate. The smiling eyes of a warm-hearted senorita made him captive, and he abandoned the gold-fields for a happy married life with the woman of his choice. An Indian guided him to this valley of green pastures in the heart of the mountain, the pine trees allured him and so here he established his ranch, stocking it with horses and cattle, and conducting it in a manner that for years has made it one of the model ranches of Southern California. A large family of boys and girls came to bless the happy couple, but now they are all grown up and scattered save one, the youngest daughter, her father's pride and joy. He says she is "his lady, cowboy, musician, and cook." Happy the father with such a daughter, and blessed the daughter with such a father.

This ranch-house has seen not a few noted literary people. Here Helen Hunt Jackson rested while on her tours of investigation of the condition of the Indians of Southern California, and many another has come to hear from the kind-hearted lady of the house stories of the early days "before the gringo came."

It is with the regret we always feel that we leave this hospitable home and tramp along through the rich pasture dotted here and there with pines. There are five meadow-valleys like this on Mount San Jacinto, but this is by far the largest and most important. It has an average altitude of four thousand four hundred feet and includes about two thousand acres, all of which is available for pasture. The water supply comes on the north from a high ridge that is an offshoot from Tauquitch Peak, and on the south from the Thomas Mountain. The meadows contain a large amount of wiregrass (*Juncus mexicanus*) and also such grasses as *Agropyron caninum, Elymus triticoides*, and *Polypogon monspeliensis*. How the cattle can eat grasses with such ponderous names and not suffer internally is a mystery, yet they seem to thrive abundantly.

An all-day's tramp is ahead of us. Clouds gather and rain begins to fall, however, before we reach the welcome shelter of the Vandeventer ranch, where kind hospitality always greets us.

It is a bright sunshiny morning that invigorates and stimulates us as we leave Vandeventer's and, swinging sharply around to the left, take the trail that leads us northeast to the desert. Hitherto we have been traveling southwest. Vandeventer's is the apex of the triangle, and we have to journey in as straight a line as mountain valleys and canyons will allow us to Palm Springs, where, if one were to draw a line across to our starting point at San Jacinto, we should find the west corner of the base line of our irregular triangle.

The trail is kindly towards us. In the main it is good, and from an elevation of 4,549 feet at the point where we leave the wagon-road it gently descends to 3,500 feet and then 2,500 in Little Paradise Valley. Now we come to the flats adorned with cottonwoods and mesquites, these latter telling us that we are once again in the actual desert zone. And how fascinating it is to study the plant growth of the various altitudes and the different zones! We have done this for years in a desultory way, but Professor H. M. Hall, of the Botanical Department of the California State University, has done it scientifically and his monograph on the subject should be in the hands of every man who makes such a trip as this. He shows that the ordinary conditions of altitude which generally affect plant growth are materially modified here by unusual conditions, such as steepness of slope, the desert winds, avalanches, and landslides, etc.

The effect of air-currents on the plant-life of San Jacinto is peculiarly interesting. On the west and southwest the breezes are the ordinary warm currents which tend to exalt the zones of plant-life to the higher summits. On the east and northeast, where naturally one expects to find these zones differing on account of the cold winds that generally come from these quarters, the very opposite occurs. For here come up the torrid winds from the desert, forcing plant-life up, far above what we find on the west and southwest.

In some places a fierce battle is constantly being waged between opposing factors which control plant distribution. One of these is on the north side of the mountain, where, as Dr. Hall says, "on account of the steep north slopes, we should expect to see the life zones running down to very low altitudes. But opposed to this factor is that of the warm air-currents rising from the Colorado Desert. The lower edge of the timber belt, which furnishes a good indication of the results of the struggle, is seen to be extremely sinuous on these slopes, running well out on the protected sides of all ridges and spurs, but immediately retreating to higher altitudes wherever it comes around on those sides exposed to the desert winds. This would seem to indicate that the lower limits of this belt are influenced not so much by the slowly ascending air-currents as by the hot winds, since the former would tend to equalize the temperature over all that region, while the latter strike as hot, drying blasts on all exposed areas."

With discussions such as these, elicited by the varying conditions as we journey, we while away the hours. Here we rise upon a ridge, and again make a quick drop of two hundred feet or more. From the ridge we look down, and there, calm, stately, and serene, we see the first group of palms. This is the out-post, the advance guard. Higher than this they have not yet been able to come in their storming of the mountain heights. What a wonderfully interesting subject it is, this influence of altitude and climate upon the growth of plant-life! Hitherto we have been in the pines, spruces, and firs. Now we are to be with the palms, with but few of the arctic species. Yet, while we love the palms, it is with a decided feeling of regret that we gaze upon our last group of pines. There they stand, the stately trees, in a most alluring cluster, - an island of green projected, as we look up to them from below, upon the deep cobalt of the mountain sky, - and as the clear and brilliant Californian sunshine sweeps through their leafy aisles, suffusing the whole palpitating cluster with its searching and resistless radiance, the very air seems filled with the aroma of creation and life.

Now the trail swerves to the right. From all sides the mountain seems to dip towards the canyon (for we are now at the head of Palm Canyon), and also northwards towards the desert, a white sheet of level sand (so it appears) bordered by the blue line of the San Bernardino Mountains. Here is a large garden of *Yucca whippleii*, and it seems as if we might have them all the way down to the desert, but they disappear almost as suddenly as they appear, and we see them no more. Now the palm trees are more frequent. One after another, individually and in clusters, they come into sight, their tall, slender boles lifting high their golden tops, crowned with green fan-leaves and looking almost like the head-gear of Indian warriors. In this canyon and at this time, they present a grand and almost awe-inspiring aspect and we are hushed into silence and delighted adoration in their presence. Down and down we go, the merry stream singing to us all the way.

The next morning is perfect, and the air deliciously cool, for the sun, though gathering strength, is not yet a fiery god scorching all things with his gaze. The desert, therefore, is not yet awake. It is dreamy and romantic. The drowsiness of sleep is yet upon its face and in its eyes. The winds as yet are but delicate breezes playing gently with the plants and flowers as tenderly as a lover touches the tresses of his sleeping love.

I remember lunching once in Palm Canyon with my wife and daughter and two friends. We found a great granite boulder that had been washed down and over until it was perfectly smooth. It had lodged near the stream, and both before and behind it giant palms had grown, which now hold it fast in their close embrace. The fan-like leaves completely sheltered the boulder. On one side there was an open entrance while on the other the water dashed noisily by. As we sat there eating our lunch we all observed the different noises made by the water, the steady, gentle murmur of the continuous flow, with an occasional ker-plunk, ker-plunk in a deep, orotund tone, as of a stone dropped into a well. Above and around us the palms kept up their gentle rustle, and gave us bewitching changes of sunshine and shade as the great leaves swung to and fro.

As we sat there in the shadow of the palms, knowing the great silent desert was just behind us, and the towering mountain peaks just ahead, we felt full of a strange, expectant awe as if some new, great, wonderful thing might happen at any moment.

The feathery fronds of the palms shut us in from all else in the world. We were alone, alone with our own hearts and God. Nature quietly intruded, however, and sent her gentle zephyrs, odor laden, to be incense at our altar, the birds sang soothingly and restfully the message of sweet peace, and the stream came down, looked at our happiness and hurried on to babble the news to all the world outside, that we were hidden in a place of joy, beauty, peace, and rest.

We returned to Palm Springs in the early afternoon, and, as we approached the settlement, it was a picture that would have charmed George Innes or William Keith. There, half a mile away, stretched a long lane, bordered on the right by fluffy looking cottonwoods of a soft pea-green, and on the left by peppers of a much deeper, richer shade. Both tones were wonderfully accentuated by the two cypress trees which form Dr. Murray's gate-way. They seemed dark to blackness compared with the lighter green of the cottonwoods and peppers. The houses, white-gabled and red-roofed, were snugly ensconced under the sheltering protection of trees, the deep colors of the oranges and figs contrasting deliciously with the predominating soft pea-greens of the cottonwoods. To the left was the dark, somber, reddish slope of the San Jacinto foot-hills, with a rude nose or promontory bathed in sunlight setting forth in brilliancy the elevated stretch of desert beyond, upon which the brownish green patches of verdure were dotted. Still farther away reached the lower hills of the Sierra San Bernardino, dimpled and shadowed, seamed and canyoned, reddish gray and deepest purple, with their rugged and irregular summits clean cut as a cameo against a cloudless Southern California desert sky.

And coming back to this oasis, as I have done several times after weeks of weary travel on the wide expanse of desolation beyond, how sweet and blessed it all is! The leaves of the trees, with the waxen blossoms of the orange and lemon, or the blushing blossoms of the almond and apricot, touch one as with tender hands bathed in sweetest perfume. The waters of its tiny creeks whisper of the cooling draughts they will give to mind as well as body. The gentle zephyrs kiss one's face and lips and hands as in tenderest caress, and the skin the fierce desert sun and winds have tanned and scorched is soothed and refreshed. Yet it is not all external, what the oasis gives. The heart beats easier, the pulses are less strong and masterful, the nerves are more under control, and the inward fever of body and brain seems quenched almost as soon as one reclines under the shade of the oasis. And then, penetrating farther, mind and soul are soothed and quieted, and one is able to see how to use the added strength and rugged power he has absorbed from the rude and uncouth, but loving and generous bosom of the desert mother.

Appendix C

From Palm to Pine

(Riverside Daily Press, *January 31, 1913)*

The glory of California's mountains has been told in song and story, lauded by brush and camera, so many times that their fame is known far and near throughout the land. This is true of all of them with one single exception—Mount San Jacinto. Like children of rich inheritance, the others have received their rightful legacy in liberal and fairly divided apportionment. But, for San Jacinto, there has been nothing but cold neglect. Is he the black sheep of the family? Those who know him love his fine massive body, wearing proudly on his noble head the silver crown of snow. Those who love him watch the light of the morning, when it transforms the silent white sheet into flaming Alpine-glow; they wait for the moon to play with softly gleaming rays on the spotless shroud enwrapping his sleeping form. All dwellers on the desert pay him homage as guardian of their domain, patron saint and protector against cold and wind, clouds and storms. During hot summer days he beckons with well-kept promises of cool glens in shaded pine-groves where springs and fresh waters bring joy to the heart of dried-out desert folk.

At Palm Springs in the shade of a palm tree, we decided to climb to the sky-line of the San Jacinto range from the desert side. It had not been done before by white people, although the oldest Indians say they used to go to Tahquitz valley straight up from the desert, an impossible feat as anyone viewing the rock-ribbed flank of the mountain would declare. We—Dr. R. L. Hill of Oakland, Morgan Draper of New York,[1] and the writer—rolled up our blankets, took provisions for three days, coffee, sugar, bread and bacon, and left Palm Springs on the second day of May. We selected as the seemingly easiest approach to the mountain the ridge between West Fork of Palm canyon and Murray canon running in a westerly direction. Our object was to find out whether a trail could be established which would connect the desert with the mountains, a trail from palm to pine.

The gentle slope, however, became steep and steeper, the packs on our shoulders heavier, our canteens lighter, and the sinking sun reminded us to make camp for the night. Into the bottom of Murray canyon we descended, where soon our camp-fire told the surprised coyotes that they were welcome to enjoy the pleasant odor of frying bacon. Early morning saw us again on the ridge, climbing over and around boulders and brush when Draper, who was in the lead, suddenly exclaimed: "Look?" He stood on a sharp ledge opposite which, at a distance of about 500 yards, was revealed a splendid spectacle of falling water, a succession of cascades of which the two largest ones were about 60 feet high. The sight reminded me of a prophetic passage in a half-forgotten railway folder: "A Yosemite may be hidden in the folds of these desert mountains."

Draper Falls. we christened the cataract, and went on our way rejoicing, meeting again and again cascades and falls of more or less height, till our attention was called to the snowcapped peak above us and the question had to be decided which ridge to choose to gain the crest. Our route was continually interrupted by unforeseen cross-canyons and mountain walls. We had passed through different zones of vegetation—first through the territory of cactus, mesquite and greasewood, then through the region of the wild plum with different varieties of juniper and bastard cedar. And now we entered the belt of dense underbrush, buckthorn and shrub oak, the latter especially showing grim determination not to let us pass.

Our hand axe was of no use; we had to throw the weight of our bodies against the brush; and, when the ranks of our foe closed so tightly together that no jackrabbit could pass through the thicket, then we climbed on top and scrambled ahead as well as we could, dropping sometimes from the top of the higher brush down to the lower. Evening came; one of our canteens had enough water left to boil coffee for the night and morning. We found a stony ledge, wide enough or rather hardly wide enough, to spread our blankets. Then camp-fire, bacon sizzling in the frying pan, the smoke of the festive pipe, fun and laughter!

The "top of the morning" saw us again on top of the scrub oak. But soon we gained the open, and reached the first snow under the first pine. Here we washed and rested, looking deep down to where, 5000 feet below our feet, lay the desert gleaming golden in the morning sun. Out of the sand rose purple hills, and faintly blue shone the placid lake of the desert, the Salton Sea. Then, moving on we waded through hard snow banked up from four to six feet, and we did not mind breaking through once in a while—it was part of the game. At noon we reached the crest of the range at an altitude of 7520 feet. Turning our face to the east, we saw the panorama of the desert; to the west, the panorama of green mountains, the Hemet reservoir, San Jacinto valley, Elsinore lake, and the far-off ocean. Tahquitz mountain and Marion mountain were at our right; but, towering above them, 10,508 feet in elevation, throned in silent icy majesty under a cold blue sky, was the mountain king, San Jacinto.

We descended in a southerly direction, toward a pasture and ranch house, which we had spied from above and which proved to be the Onstott ranch, the goal we had intended to make. Walking on top of trees was now a mere joke; and, after two hours of crawling through heavy undergrowth and dropping from thicket into thicket, we came at last into the valley and set foot on solid ground, strolling over pastures green where gentle cows grazed, a pastoral scene that set dreams afloat of milk and honey. No need to say that we found friendly hospitality at the ranch house, that our dreams were realized—milk and honey, and bread with apples to boot. In fine spirits we again took to the road, which led us over verdant fields studded with stately pine trees. Night overtook us but light broke through the darkness—Keen Kamp! Here we felt at home at once. To be in good company, to enjoy good meals, to sit around a cozy fire—what pleasure.

The next day we took a "pasear" to Idyllwild, the romantic summer resort among pines and oaks; and, after another night spent at Keen Kamp, we entered the home stretch through Thomas valley to the old Vandewenter ranch and down the Vandewenter trail to Palm canyon—the desert—Palm Springs. From the West.

[1.] Dr. R. L. Hill is Dr. Robert Hill, a general practice physician in Oakland. Morgan Draper was originally born in New York but in the 1910 census is listed as a civil and mining engineer living in San Rafael, California (1910 U. S. Federal Census, Ancestry.com).

Appendix D

From Pines to Palms on the Gordon Trail

(Riverside Daily Press, *August 15, 1917)*

Starting from Idyllwild, one takes the short trail, known as the Devil's Slide, of three miles, and arrives on top of a mighty mass of rock and finds a beautiful table land, known as the Tauquitz valley, lying between Tauquitz peak and Marion mountain.

Here the trail leads past the log cabin into Hidden Lake trail, or until you reach Mr. Law's trail, and across Willow creek. Now there is nothing but an old deer trail until one comes out on a little bit of flat ground on Tauquitz creek, just as the creek takes its first tumble of some 40 feet, down towards the desert, which is nearly 6000 feet below.

This is "Camp Caramba," where M. S. Gordon has a charming camp site, and it is from this point that Mr. Gordon has built his trail winding down to the desert.

Starting first up over a high point, with a most wonderful view of the Coachella valley, then among the noble pines, you start down the mountain past Sentinel Point, on down to McInnis peak, passing from trees to shrubs, finally to cactus and rocks.

One sees the new auto road leading from Palm Springs to Indian Wells almost directly beneath, but the trail leads on down to the log-back between Tauquitz canyon and one of the north forks of Andreas canyon, leading south below McInnis peak for a mile or two, then up over the saddle and down again nearing Andreas canyon, winding down amongst curiously shaped rocks, the Imp and Dog's Head being most prominent, until you finally land at Camp Avispas, meaning wasps, due to the many wasp nests among the cactus.

This is the last water supply before reaching the desert. Also at this point you see your first group of palm trees, which is at an altitude of about 2000 feet.

From Camp Avispas the trail leads on, bringing you closer to the desert at every step, with a most wonderful view of the palisades of Andreas canyon, and her wonderful groups of plams in their long petticoats.

This trail from pines to palms is the first direct connection between the desert of the Coachella valley and the mountain resort of Idyllwild, as the crow flies, some 12 miles, but one goes slowly, climbing the distance up over a point 8000 feet, and should allow on horseback, going up, at least 12 or 13 hours, including an hour to rest and water your horse at Camp Caramba.

Always have we been told that a trail over this country was impossible, but this saying did not daunt Mr. Gordon, who worked it out during the past year, with Mr. McInnis to help him, and at an expense of about $1000.

This is the only location in the United States where all the growths of different zones are represented in such a short distance, from desert up to San Jacinto peak, nearly 11,000 feet, from the desert sands with cactus and palms to the snowy regions with pines and firs.

The "Pines and Palms Trails" of Wonders

by George Law
(Los Angeles Times, *October 3, 1920)*

California possesses what Prof. McAdie of Harvard, formerly of the weather bureau, calls an adjustable climate, "meaning thereby that the climate seeker can find the climate he desires and, indeed, have his choice of climates according to his desire."

There is a summary of this fact available in the course of a single day's outing on a trail in Riverside county little known as yet to the nature loving public. It is appropriately called the "Pines and Palms Trail," taking out from the lair of the wild palm in the Colorado Desert and ascending in twelve not too difficult miles to the habitat of the pine.

Probably nowhere else in the world, certainly nowhere else in North America, does there exist a combination of conditions - climatic, botanical, scenic - so varied and opposite within so few miles. The austral influence hobnobs with the boreal, aridity and fecundity lie side by side; below there is a waterless waste; above an elysium of meadows, forests and dells.

This amazing juxtaposition of zones ordinarily separated by thousands of miles, is owing to the peculiarities of one mountain. You may catch visionary glimpses of this solitary mountain from points along the boulevards of Southern California; or you may see it piercing the sky as you crawl up the desert from Imperial Valley. Its name is San Jacinto. No doubt you recall how Ramona and Allesandro were caught in a snowstorm while seeking a haven of refuge on the slopes of Mt. San Jacinto. It stands, an everlasting barrier, between the fairest acres in the world and the most desolate. From a narrow base in the primeval Gulf of California it piles skyward, sheer, tremendous, awe-inspiring, far more than two zenith miles. The heat of the desert has been so fierce and persistent as to have singed the granite of the lower buttresses and walls to a chocolate brown. Yet the air above is rarified and chilled, and winter packs the forested ledges with masses of snow. Three atmospheres meet and blend; from the west comes the moist semitropic breath of the ocean, only sixty miles distant; from the east the dry winds of the desert; these temporize with the ever-present Alpine air, creating the most ideal blend of climate imaginable.

Ice Cold Springs on Heights
Boiling Hot in Valley.

Up and down the slopes the changes are registered in plant and animal life, in the rocks and topography, in the air and moisture, even in the temperature of the water. For at the foot of the mountain are many hot springs, while the lovely meadows and forests above abound with springs and streams of icy coldness.

Some of the enchanting variety was available from the west side of the mountain, where several summer resorts, roads and trails render access easy. But not until the making of the "Pines and Palms Trail" were the features of most contrast and wonder opened to the inspection and study of recreation seekers. This trail was in the order of a remarkable achievement. Heretofore the east side of the mountain had never been scaled. To reach the heights, but a few miles by airline above the sentiments of the desert, a journey of fifty miles to the other side of the mountain was required. The Forest Service, whether because of the precipitousness of the slope or the absence of timber, was uninterested. It remained for an enthusiastic resident of Palm Springs and Idyllwild, Mr. M. S. Gordon, to put through the undertaking, thus connecting his two domiciles by a short cut over the mountain, and presenting the public with the possibility of an excursion of unparalleled interest. Nearly everywhere the inaccessibility of the rocky slopes, sheer walls, spillways, crags and deeply cleft canyons, is only too apparent. It was Mr. Gordon's self-appointed task to find a way where to the eye and comprehension no way existed. The task took two years, working down from the groves of pines by summer, and up from the palmy jungles by winter. Shreds of rags and piles of stones still bear witness to the difficult and hazardous climbs made by the old gentleman in laying out the course. Fully cognizant of the wonders between Palm Springs and Idyllwild, he entertained, and realized, the dream of uniting the two by a direct trail traversable in a day.

One sets out horseback or afoot from the oasis town of Palm Springs. The desert - sand and creosote, with occasional palo verdes and smoke-bushes - stretches away in three directions, with the burnt buttresses of Mt. San Jacinto in the fourth - and fifth! The way leads through the Garden of Eden, once luxuriant with herbage and soft delights (so 'tis told;) now a dessicated spot with nary a sign of apple tree. Turning from the desert into a canyon mouth, one comes upon a veritable jungle of palms, desert-willows, mesquite and wild grape.

Southern California is almost as well known for tamed palms as for oranges. But few people realize that the palm can be found here in its wild condition. There is something startling, even weird, in coming upon a group of these shaggy foreigners hidden away in a rocky crevice of the desert hills. One is accustomed to them in stately trimmed-up rows along the avenues. Here they defy order and have their full hoop-skirts on. And then the sound of the desert wind in the palm leaves! It is exotic, Arabian. One expects next to meet up with turbaned outlaws.

From the lair of the palm the trail ascends the mountain slope, first through a barren region dedicated to rock and cholla. The cholla is one of the most beautifully bristling varieties of cactus. It grows to some height and branches like a bush. Globular segments of forbiddingness drop off and accumulate in the trail, from which it is not wise to attempt to kick them. Barrel-cacti are prominent also, affording refreshing thought to one acquainted with the legend of their watery content. A few other cacti, several yuccas, cat-claw and wild apricot bushes thrive in the desert garden, all putting forth blooms of unsuspected beauty in the spring of the year.

The trail then enters the chaparral belt where a variety of mountain bushes hide the rocks and change gray brownness to sea green. First the red-shank, or imitation cedar, dominates. This is a near relative of the chamiso greasewood, so abundant in all the mountains of the Southland. But the red-shank possesses the distinction suggested by this rude name, grows tall and free, and its cedarlike foliage gives off a delicate peppery aroma, very like the scent of violets when brought out by a summer shower. Next comes the kingdom of the manzanita, a better known and more widely distributed shrub. It is the little apple bush, productive of seedy berries relished by the Indians for meal, and by camping housewives for jelly. By the time one reaches the manzanita the canteen may be quite dry. The acid berries will do much to relive thirst. Indeed, they are often used to make a most refreshing beverage.

Mingling with the manzanita in ever-increasing abundance are oak brush, mountain mahogany, dwarf buckthorn and chinquapin. These accompany the climber to the habitat of the pine. The dwarf buckthorn affords favorite pasture for the deer. To wearied human beings it suggests the comfort of a readymade box-spring mattress, but disillusionment comes quickly, for the thorn part is no idle fancy.

Before dipping with the "Pines and Palms Trail" into the wild elysium of the heights, one is impelled to pause a few minutes on the rim and to gaze desertward. In the many breathing spells all along the trail, one has feasted upon the immensely open, and ever more immensely open view. But as the desert recedes, so does its reality, until from the rim a new and strange world is spread out below. In coloring and topography it must be like the surface of the moon. There are none of the warm hospitable tones contributed by moisture and a humid atmosphere. Everywhere the fantastic landscape is dazzlingly bright and bare. The many hued desert clays and sands blend in a saffron sheen, unearthly, uncomforting. The Salton Sea gleams with metallic intensity. One knows that the region was never intended for the habitation of man. Spectacular it is, and indeed why should not this be enough? For there is a fascination and a clearing of the mental and spiritual eye in gazing upon it.

All is Beauty Here on the
Top o' the World.

Convinced that one is on the top of the world, with a sigh of content at being there, one turns to the comforts and beauties near at hand.

Here is a sylvan paradise, known to and feared by the Indians as the realm of Tahquitz, an evil spirit. Clever this spirit to appropriate what every visitor is ready to agree is the rarest, gentlest, most exquisite wilderness safe from exploitation by modern man. No one can enter it without hazard and effort. No one can tarry there for long at a time. All that is naturally beautiful and beneficent is present; what is artificially so is absent. Man can introduce nothing ugly, except the gun in deer season. Nature does not do so, unless lightning play and flying snow are so to be classed.

There are about twenty-four square miles of ledge ranging in altitude from 7000 to 10,000 feet. All of this is forested with many varieties of pine. Two good-sized creeks with numerous tributaries flow through the region. There is one lake, surprisingly situated in a balcony of rock upon the brink of the desert declivity. Springs abound in the dells, ravines and meadows. In places there is dense underbrush - wild cherry, black willow, service berry and wild currant in company with the usual mountain bushes. Here the abundant deer have their secret passages to places of refuge from the hunter. Several large glades and numerous small ones realize all that is most beautiful in fancies of Arcadian meadows. Only they are hushed in the mystery of nonhuman intrusion.

The balmy caresses of summer arouse a response transporting to the senses. Gently slopes and cool spaces of the forest are quickly overgrown with brake ferns. Giant lupins, lilies, and brilliant fireweeds rise among them. The growth is tall, luxuriant - a person is a pigmy wading through a sea of fresh verdure and rich color. The dells become exquisite bowers festooned and draped with innumerable vines and flowers. Bevies of azaleas crowd the brooksides and fill the air with fragrance. Columbines lean gracefully out over the sparkling, murmuring water. Even on dry ridges the flowers thrive, nourished by showers bestowed only upon this paradise. There is a succession of color schemes; first the lavender and silver of lupins; next the yellow of wallflowers; then scarlet bugler red, and finally goldenrod gold. There are of course many other flowers, though growing in less profusion - Catalina mariposas, potentillas, monoradellas, paint brushes, pink everlasting, the rich and gorgeous purple-blooming sage. To classify them all is a task of several seasons.

Unique Pilgrim is Flower of the Mint Family

Odd to relate, one little flower of the mint family has wandered down the mountainside from the Alpine to the Sonoran zone. This unique pilgrim has modified his form to suit the altered conditions. He is a fine advertisement for self-adaptation as the secret of success. Yet his changes are not so radical as to obscure his identity, nor to class his three slightly different selves as distinct species.

But this monoradella is the only adventurer. The flowers and plants of Tahquitz belong to the race of moisture-loving mountaineers. Across the dreary wastes of the desert their brothers and first cousins are blooming in the great Rockies.

At the palm end of the trail the type of plant life is diametrically different; fresh green gives way to ash, sage, dull olive; leaves contract to stems, spikes and spines; no longer luxuriant denizens of Elysian Fields, the stragglers of the desert are fantastic caricatures of plant life.

The antithesis is just as marked in the animal world. Above are deer, foxes, squirrels, birds, butterflies - true nymphs and dryads of a supernal wilderness; below, little besides such creeping things as love to bask in the torrid sunshine and warm their bellies upon rocks shimmering with waves of heat.

Not that the contrast discredits the desert. It is an opposition of difference merely, without jealousy as to the extent of interest and the amount of beauty.

What is beautiful and interesting depends, finally, upon the individual. The "Pines and Palms Trail" is a way of wonders fraught with the riches sort of entertainment for the lover of the wild. That one man prefers a palm-leaf hut beside a hot spring at the foot of the mountain, that another elects to dwell in a rock cabin upon the heights, are not so much rival declarations as to beauty, as testimony of the excellencies of both scenes.

Appendix E

Fulmor's 1921 Report on Palm Canyon Road

(as reported in both the Hemet News *and Indio* Date Palm, *April 30, 1926)*

To the Honorable Board of Supervisors, of the County of Riverside, Riverside, California

February 17, 1921

Gentlemen:

As per your order, I have made a reconnaissance for a road from Keen Camp to Palm Springs via Hemet valley, Vandeventer Flat and Palm canyon, and would report that it is entirely feasible to build a good road over this route, with grades not exceeding 5 or 6 per cent, at an estimated cost of $80,000.

The distance, as estimated from Keen Camp to the end of the present road in Palm canyon, is estimated at 35 miles. Of this amount 15 miles from Keen Camp to Vandeventer Flat is open for travel at the present time, and is a very fair mountain road, with few exceptions. It is estimated that with the expenditure of $4,500 this portion could be put in good condition for travel.

From Vandeventer Flat, the route of the road as examined, would lie along the west side of Palm canyon and for a distance of four miles would have to be built over a rough, rocky country. The cost of which I have estimated at $7,500 per mile.

From a point south of the junction of Palm canyon and Onstott creek, the road would extend down the bottom of Palm canyon, following approximately the route of the present traveled trail, to a junction with the present road from Palm Springs to Palm canyon, near the north boundary of Section 14, township 5 south, range 4 east, S. B. M. This section of the road would be approximately 13 miles in length and the cost is estimated at $3,500 per mile, making the total length 35 miles, and the total estimated cost $80,000.

From Keen Camp, at an elevation of 4,700 feet, the route would extend southeasterly over the present traveled road to the summit of the divide between Hurky creek and Johnson creek at an elevation of 4936 feet. Thence southeasterly along the present traveled road, to the Hemet valley, at an elevation of 4394 feet; thence continuing up the Hemet valley over approximately the present traveled route, to the summit of the divide between Hemet valley and Vandeventer Flat, at an elevation of 4985 feet, and a distance from Keen Camp of 14.6 miles.

From Hurky creek, at the northerly end of the Hemet valley, there is an almost imperceptible grade up the valley to the divide just noted. The route then follows easterly across the Vandeventer Flat on easy grades, to the head of Palm canyon, 18 miles from Keen Camp, at an elevation of 4550 feet. This portion of the road would be located on decomposed granite soil, on which a road would be well drained, cheaply constructed and easily maintained.

The first four miles at the head of Palm canyon, as noted, would be located over a very rough and rocky country, there being very little soil on the surface. It would be necessary to blast the road almost entirely out of solid rock.

From the mouth of Onstott creek, the road would extend along the benches in the bottom or sides of Palm canyon.

The side slopes would be small, and it would be necessary to move very little dirt in the construction of the road. Rock extends close to the surface, however, and that portion of the road constructed in fill would probably be more cheaply built by being retained by a wall of loose rock, owing to a scarcity of dirt to make the fill and complete the surface of the road bed.

A fair quantity of water rises in Palm canyon at numerous places in sufficient quantities for travelers and domestic use.

The elevation of the road at its northern terminus at the junction of the present road in Palm canyon would be approximately 700 feet. From this point to the village of Palm Springs, the distance is approximately six miles.

With the exception of approximately four miles at the head of Palm canyon, the road would offer little difficulty in its construction.

                    Respectfully,

                    A. C. Fulmor

                    County Surveyor

Appendix F

Fulmor's Report on Pinon Pines Road

(as reprinted in the Indio Date Palm, June 22, 1928)

Riverside, California
March 10, 1928

Honorable Board of Supervisors
Of Riverside County, California,
Gentlemen:

As requested by your Honorable Board, I have made an examination and survey to determine the cost of building a road from the present end of the pavement in Section 20, Township 5 South, Range 6 East, S. B. B. & M., up Dead Indian Creek to Pinon Flats on the north side of the Santa Rosa Mountains and report as follows:

The route as examined and surveyed begins at the west end of the pavement between Indio and Palm Springs in the center of the west line of Section 20, Township 5 South, Range 6 East, S. B. B. & M., and extends southerly up the broad gravel wash of Dead Indian Creek to a point near the junction of Carrizo Creek, thence southeasterly over low hills to a divide at an elevation of fifteen hundred (1500) feet between Carrizo Creek and Deep Canyon in the southeast quarter of Section 7, Township 6 South, Range 6 East, S.B.B. & M. The line then turns southwest to Carrizo creek at the present trail, where it turns in a Northeasterly direction to the top of the ridge between Carrizo and Deep Canyon, up which it follows in a southerly direction and swings around the east side of Black Hill above the present trail. From Black Hill the route should follow in a southwesterly direction up gently sloping ground to Pinon Flats in the northeast quarter of Section 34, Township 6 South, Range 5 East, S.B.B. & M., at an elevation of approximately four thousand two hundred and fifty (4250) feet.

Topography

Section 1. On the section from the paved highway to the foot of the grade in Section 7, Township 6 South Range 6 East, S.B.B. & M., four (4) miles in length, the road follows up a broad valley over a gravelly soil. Practically no cutting or filling will be necessary in this section to make the roadway. After the desert brush is broken by a railroad rail and the brush burned, the road can be made with a grader and drag. The soil and gravel is so graded in uniformity that an excellent roadbed can be made in nearly this entire section from the natural materials.

Owing to limited time and funds and the cheap cost of construction no detailed survey was made of this section.

Section 2. The section from the foot of the hill at Carrizo Creek to the pass in the southeast quarter of Section 7, Township 6 South, Range 6 East, S.B.B. & M., at fifteen hundred (1500) feet elevation - between Carrizo and Deep Canyon – one and one-half miles in length passes over low hills at the foot of the main Mountain. The cross slope of the ground is small averaging about 25 feet per hundred. Decomposed rock - a gneiss of schist - is exposed on the surface over a large part of this section, and loose boulders averaging one to two feet in dimension are strewn over the surface. The excavation is light in this section averaging only 7000 cubic yards per mile.

Section 3. The section from the pass at fifteen hundred (1500) feet elevation to the top of the ridge near the center of Section 18, Township 6 South, Range 6 East, S.B.B. & M., between Carrizo and Deep Canyon, three (3) miles in length crosses the roughest and steepest country on the route. The decomposed rock is exposed at the surface over practically this entire section and loose boulders over about two (2) miles. The excavation averages 13,000 cubic yards per mile on this Section.

Section 4. From the top of the ridge near the center of Section 18, to the southwesterly side of Black Hill one and nine-tenths (1.9) miles, the route follows in a general way except around Black Hill, the crest between Carrizo Creek and Deep Canyon. Decomposed rock is exposed on the surface on only a portion of this section and the excavation is comparatively light averaging 6000 cubic yards per mile. Where the road follows the slope of Black Hill for a distance of four tenths (4/10) miles, loose boulders one to four feet in dimensions cover the side hill rather thickly.

Section 5. From Black Hill to Pinon Flats, five (5) miles, the road would follow over a rolling surface sloping east to Deep Canyon. The side slope is small and will average ten (10) to fifteen (15) feet per hundred. The soil is a decomposed granite that will make an excellent road bed. Very little rock is exposed at the surface on this section, and the greater part of the excavation for the road will be earth. No detailed survey was made of this section owing to the cheap cost of construction and lack of time and money.

Grades and Alignment

Section 1. The grade on Section 1, from the Highway, four miles up the broad valley of Dead Indian Canyon to Carrizo Creek is approximately four per cent.

Section 2. From Carrizo Creek to the pass at an elevation of fifteen hundred feet, one and one-half miles, the ruling grade is six per cent, with many stretches of so called "resting grades" varying from level to four per cent on which automobiles may pick up speed.

Section 3. From the pass at fifteen hundred feet elevation to the top of the ridge between Carrizo Creek and Deep Canyon – three (3) miles – the ruling grade is six per cent. There is three quarters (3/4) of a mile eight per cent grade on the lower end of this section caused by lack of room to develop the necessary distance at a reasonable expense on a lower grade. There are several stretches of "resting grades" on this section, which is true also of the other sections.

Section 4. From the top of the ridge near the center of Section 18 to the southwesterly side of Black Hill, one and nine tenths (1.9) miles the ruling grade is six per cent with a maximum of seven per cent for a short distance.

Section 5. From Black Hill to Pinon Flats, five (5) miles, the ruling grade is five per cent. Owing to the favorable topography on this section for road building, any grade, desirable up to ten or twelve per cent may be laid out. Steeper grades than five per cent will shorten the road in direct proportion to the increase in grade.

This report is based on a roadway sixteen (16) feet wide. When not traveling at a high rate of speed, two automobiles can pass each other on this width with safety.

A few curves have been laid out on a maximum radius of one hundred and fifty (150) feet but in general two hundred (200) feet is the minimum radius of curvature used on this survey. On this alignment it is practical to widen the road to care for increased traffic in the future.

From the proposed terminus on the east side of Pinon Flats this road can be cheaply extended southwesterly across Pinon Flats, to Vandeventer Flats and Hemet Valley, Keen Camp and Idyllwild. There is now a wagon track, over which it is possible to drive an automobile from Pinon Flats to Vandeventer Flats. There is now in use a road from Vandeventer Flats down the Hemet Valley to Keen Camp. Very little work has ever been done on this road, and it is merely a track for one vehicle. A satisfactory road can be built at a small cost.

Pinon Flats lies on the north side of the Santa Rosa Mountains at an altitude of four thousand (4000) to forty-five hundred (4500) feet and covers an area of several thousand acres. It is on the desert side of the main coast range of mountains, and has a dry atmosphere. The summer days are hot, but the nights are comparatively cool as might be expected at this altitude. The water supply at present is limited to a few springs on the south slope of the Santa Rosa Mountain. The altitude and exposure of the north slope of the Santa Rosa Mountain indicates that proper conservation methods can make available a greatly increased supply. It is covered with a growth of pinon pines, which trees bear the pine nuts for sale in our stores. These trees range from twelve (12) to eighteen (18) inches in diameter and fifteen (15) to twenty-five (25) feet in height, however they are too small and scraggly to afford much shade.

This route affords a wonderful view of the San Jacinto, Santa Rosa, and San Bernardino Mountains over the greater portion of its length. At a few points on the road, Salton Sea can be seen on the distant horizon and a magnificent panorama of the Coachella Valley is in view for a long distance.

As a scenic route for tourist travel it has much to recommend, but it is its practical value to the people of Coachella, Palo Verde and Imperial Valleys which deserves the greater consideration. The building of this road will shorten the distance between the centers of population in the Coachella Valley and mountain recreational areas, so much that its location will enable a great many of the people of Coachella Valley to sleep in a cooler climate while carrying on their daily work. It will serve the residents of Palm Springs as well as the Coachella Valley, and as highway traffic increases will become a main route for travel through the southern part of Riverside county, to Hemet and San Diego County. Its building will shorten the distance between the Coachella Valley and Beach resorts in San Diego County, twenty six (26) miles.

Estimate of Cost of Sixteen Foot Roadway from Palm Springs – Indio Highway to Pinon Flats

Highway to Carrizo Creek, 4 miles at per mile **$500.00**	**$2,000.00**
Carrizo Creek to Black Hill, 6.4 miles (Surveyed) 70,000 cu. yd. excavation at $.70 **$49,000.00**	
Culverts **$7,500.00**	**$56,500.00**
Black Hill to Pinon Flats Five (5) miles at per mile **$3,000.00**	**$15,000.00**
Engineering	**$5,000.00**
Total	**$76,500.00**

The distance from Pinon Flats to Van Deventer Flats is estimated at eight (8) miles and the estimated cost of a sixteen (16) foot road at $3,500.00 per mile.

The route as examined is feasible and practical in cost, and I believe will serve the different communities interested better than any other route.

Respectfully yours,
A. C. Fulmor
County Surveyor

Appendix G

HIGHWAY MAY GIRDLE MOUNTAIN; OFFICIALS TRAVERSE PROPOSED ROUTES
San Jacinto and Santa Rosa Mountains To Be Linked With Desert Spaces By Proposed Road, Remote Districts Are Explored

by Jessica Bird
(Riverside Daily Press, *April 18, 1929)*

That an automobile highway encircling the San Jacinto mountains may become an actuality within the next few years is the hope of those who long have dreamed of the project, since an exploration of two proposed routes for the extension of the present road from mountain heights to desert valleys has just been accomplished by county, state, and federal authorities.

Traveling territory that can be reached at present only on horseback or afoot, the party of officials, under the guidance of Idyllwild, Palm Springs, and Coachella valley residents sponsoring the trip, last night completed a three day tour of the San Jacinto and Santa Rosa mountain slopes.

It is conceded that this journey will prove the first step toward a road-building program of immense importance to all Southern California.

All who made the trip expressed a deepened interest in the project, and the opinion that it is entirely feasible to circle the towering San Jacinto mountain range with a tourist highway. It is possible that still other routes may be sought with a view to shortening the road before any definite determination is reached by the county supervisors, or action taken by the state or federal authorities. Deep satisfaction was evident among the sponsors of the exploration, however, in the evident interest displayed by officials.

Leaving Riverside Monday afternoon, those making up the party gathered at Idyllwild Inn, where they were guests for the night. The county supervisors took occasion Monday afternoon to visit the prison camp, which was found in excellent condition, and to show the visiting road officials the progress being made on the construction of the high-gear boulevard from Hemet to Idyllwild, to be opened for use this year.

Early Tuesday morning the party left Idyllwild by automobile, going to Keen Camp, and thence via Herkey creek, Garner's ranch, and Kenworthy to Vandeventer Flats, where saddle horses brought from Palm Springs. Here the real journey began, and roads were left behind for trails.

Santa Rosa peak, lifting its snow-capped head 8000 feet, was the commanding point. The trail led from the little Indian reservation at Vandeventer's across ravines which ran into the precipitous canyons of the lower ranges. Pinon flats stretched away from the right hand, as the party turned in a northerly direction and made for the head of Palm canyon. Soon the view of the desert and the towering peak of Mt. San Jacinto, with its snowy white companions, Tahquitz and Marion peaks, was visible. The magnificence of the panorama was impressive.

The down-hill route through Palm canyon, a distance of fully 15 miles by the trail followed, presented a diversity of views. Chalk-white limestone hills marked the remnant of a mountain so ancient that the massive red-hued walls of the canyon immediately opposite seemed unbelievably young and crude in their formation. Water flowed from the side canyons to join the main stream, and before many miles had been crossed the first wild palm trees were glimpsed. They grew deep in a ravine walled perfectly by cliffs, and marked a water seepage.

The stop for luncheon (which had been provided by Hobart Garlick of the Oasis Hotel at Palm Springs), was made by the side of a stream where cienega-willows and scraggling mesquites formed a thicket. Marks of the canyon flood of 3 years ago were plainly visible, debris being piled many feet high against trees which had withstood the torrents.

Desert plants and cacti were blooming, and delicate flowers, springing up from the sand, were seen along the trail. Barrel cacti wore golden crowns of bloom. No mountain sheep were seen by the party, but they are known to frequent the region and are often seen in considerable herds. Much of the territory hereabouts is in the game reserve.

Resuming the trip in the afternoon, the cavalcade continued along the route of Palm canyon, sometimes deep in the canyon and traversing sides of steep hills. The horses were excellent, the urge to "move on" was apparent, and before 2 o'clock Tuesday afternoon, the party had reached the better known part of the canyon, where hundreds of palms in groves showed green and brown among the red rocks of the ravines. At one point, where the trail zig-zagged along the face of a hill, two groups of palms growing nearly to the top of the range were seen, evidently bordering warm springs. Beyond the mouth of the canyon, marked by the mesa overlooking the main grove of trees and serving as a parking place for the thousands of automobiles visiting this unusual natural wonder each year, the village of Palm Springs was to be seen. Beyond this lay the desert, walled by the San Bernardino and San Jacinto mountains.

At the mouth of Palm canyon, the horses were abandoned for automobiles, which carried the party the intervening six miles from the mesa to the town. Here a welcome awaited at the Desert Inn, and the erstwhile horsemen after their unusual trip, were glad to rest.

The Palm Springs Chamber of Commerce, which includes the hotel men and merchants of the desert winter resort, with Earl Coffman as president and Phillip Boyd as executive secretary, planned details of the journey to this point in cooperation with Idyllwild Inc. owners, including Mr. and Mrs. C. L. Emerson, who accompanied the party, and Mr. and Mrs. J. O. Percival, in charge of Idyllwild Inn. Boyd was "captain" of the tour.

Mrs. Nellie N. Coffman, founder of the Desert Inn, was hostess at a dinner party for 27, including the members of the exploring party, Tuesday night. Secretary Boyd acted as toastmaster, and introduced members of the party, who expressed delight not only at the revelation offered by the trip, but also for the cordial hospitality accorded them.

Yesterday morning the party left the Desert Inn for a hurried tour about the village of Palm Springs by automobile, and then traveled over the Palm Springs-Indio county highway to a point near Indian Wells. Here the highway was left behind and over a three mile road of typical desert variety, the cars drove directly to the mouth of Carrizo canyon. Here the Dead Indian trail begins.

Coachella valley men and women representing every settlement in the valley were present in a crowd to welcome the visitors. Another string of saddle horses had been provided by the new hosts, and

*"After the first ridge had been topped . . .
both Mt. San Gorgonio and Mt. San Jacinto being seen . . ."*

within a short time the party was again well mounted and starting on the upward trail over the second proposed route.

After the first ridge had been topped the wonderful scenic possibilities of this way were also evident, both Mt. San Gorgonio and Mt. San Jacinto being seen, and the desert region mapped to apparently limitless distance. The interesting growth of cacti including hundreds of red blossoming ocotillo, was particularly marked along this route. Century plants were seen in bloom, their flowers orange-yellow, and the cholla cacti proved ubiquitous. Several of the horses picked up the thorny balls, and County Surveyor A. C. Fulmor proved himself an adept rider when his horse, frightened by the pricking of thorns, staged a wild-west show on the narrow trail atop a steep hill.

The course of the tentative survey made by the county along this so-called Pinon Flats route from the desert, which is being put forward by Coachella valley residents, was easily followed by the stakes. It kept well to the ridges, dipping down at various points to cross canyons, but for the most part choosing the high-lines. As on the trip made the day previous, the scenic possibilities of this road were most evident.

At one of the various stops made to rest the horses (and the riders!) a refreshing feast of sweet Coachella valley grapefruit, sent from the Clark ranch near Pt. Happy, was enjoyed.

Black Hill, a jagged mass of rocks, was skirted to the east. At a point near the headwaters of Carrizo creek, were found twin palm trees, making Dos Palmas springs.

Deep canyon, one of the most wonderful of the desert mountain gorges, lay between the country traversed by the trail and the Sheep mountains, which in turn were backed by the Martinez range. A short detour from the trail took the party to a point overlooking the crag of Deep canyon, and many hundreds of feet below were pockets in which palms and other trees were growing.

Perhaps more amazing than anything else on the landscape, however, was the sight of a Ford perched upon the opposite canyon rim. "We told you a car could get that far," said the Coachella valley residents who were accompanying the party, to the county officials. Wilson Howell, who has several times before made his way with a car to this point, was waiting smilingly when the horseback party arrived on the trail. He had come via Idyllwild and Vandeventer Flats to the Asbestos mountain region, and thence had broken trail to Deep canyon.

The trail crossed the immense Pinon Flats forests, the growth of this timber reaching as far as could be seen to the foot of Mt. Santa Rosa and old El Toro, a neighboring peak.

Luncheon, which was packed on the trail on a pinto pony in approved frontier style, proved an appetizing contribution from La Quinta Hotel, the manager of which, Walter Morgan, had been among the greeters in the Coachella valley group. The picnic was eaten at Asbestos Spring, where C. E. Bunker maintains a camp on a part of the immense acreage he controls. The mountaineer, formerly a Palm Springs resident, has a splendid 2100 acre ranch near Kenworthy, where the Ramona caves are to be found. He accompanied the party on both of the trail trips.

Several members of the party made another side trip from this point, going to the Asbestos Mines, in which J. O. Percival of Idyllwild is principal owner. The mine is not being operated at present.

Automobiles had been brought by John Kenna and William Mumper, who acted as official chauffeurs for the party, to the Asbestos Springs, over a perpendicular road. This road returned the crowd to Vandeventer Flats, and the remainder of the return trip down the mountain to Hemet and San Jacinto was easily accomplished.

Those included in the party over the Palm Canyon route were Supervisors T. C. Jameson, John Shaver, Harvey Johnson, J. E. McGregor, and W. C. Moore; County Surveyor A. C. Fulmor. A. E. Bottell, horticultural commissioner and secretary of the San Jacinto Mountain State Park association; E. T. Mische of the California State Park organization, a representative of Frederick Law Olmsted; F. E. Hopper, district engineer, federal forest service; Fred J. Grumm, engineer of surveys and plans, California division of highways; Supervisor J. E. Elliott, San Bernardino federal forest service; E. E. East, chief engineer, Auto Club of Southern California; E. C. Wickerd, superintendent of the Riverside county prison camp; Mr. and Mrs. C. L. Emerson of Idyllwild, Inc.; Miss Jessica Bird, Riverside Daily Press; C. E. Bunker, Geo. Roberson of Palm Springs; Robert W. Reed and William J. Westerfield, Banning Chamber of Commerce.

The majority of this party made the return trip to the mountains yesterday, being accompanied and guided by Coachella valley representatives. These included J. Win Wilson, editor of the Indio Date Palm; L. R. Hayward, Dr. and Mrs. Harry W. Smiley, Arthur L. Wood and others of Indio. Raymond Cree and Norman Farra of Palm Springs.

Appendix H

Pinon Pines Road

Indio Date Palm, *December 13, 1929*

The following article, written by someone who evidently has been over the proposed road and made a study of it, is clipped from WOMAN'S CLUB SERVICE.

The residents of Coachella valley have one great crying need – a suitable road from their valley to the nearby Santa Rosa and Santa [sic] Jacinto mountains.

They have themselves built a passable road from the pavement west of Indio up to the 1,000 foot level. They have also built from the highways on the west side of the mountain across several miles of territory to a point four miles from the lower road and less than two thousand feet above it.

Repeated trips have been made over this route, driving up from the pavements below and walking the four miles up an old Indian trail and from there taking car again for the trip over the top to the roads connecting with Keen Camp, Idyllwild, Hemet and San Jacinto or Anza, Coahuila (Cahuilla), Aguanga and Temecula. This road is in fairly good shape and can be used by experienced mountain drivers.

A highway built on this route will fill in a missing link and connect several lines of travel, opening up many possibilities of a scenic trip through the mountains and desert and in this way will serve all of Southern California.

The scenery along this route offers a great variety of attractions as one drives through the floor of the desert to the high mountain side and meadows. On leaving the Indio-Palm Springs road about twelve miles west of Indio, the route rises gently to the south, giving one an increasing view of the desert as one goes higher; after about four miles the points of desert mountains stretch out and almost surround one. The route then leaves the wash and starts up the side of one of the northern spurs – about a mile of this rocky slope and then you come out on top of this spur, the view changes and one can look down into the mouth of Deep Canyon.

Deep Canyon from the Cahuilla Tewahnet overlook

A couple of swings to the west and east with changing vistas at each turn and glimpses of a running stream in Carrizo canyon and one is on top again with a much wider view of desert and mountain and the yawning depths of Deep Canyon make a second appearance.

From this high ridge the road swings across a small flat and back again, skirting the side of the Deep Canyon gorge in order to pass Black Hill. This third and last view of Deep Canyon's most interesting gorge is one of the most scenic wonders of the entire route. One will be able to park and walk out onto the promontories that overhang the gorge and see and hear a running stream a thousand feet below; with groups of native palms and other verdure, with the expanse of Sheep Mountain on the far side.

The route then swings to the southwest and climbs to the ridge at Pinon Flats, 4,300 feet high, with the curious and beautiful little pinon pines. There one leaves temporarily the old views, which have been getting bigger and more beautiful all the while, and new vistas appear. [One can view] The whole north side of Santa Rosa mountain and the slope of Pinon Flats down to the upper reaches of Palm Canyon with the east slope of San Jacinto beyond.

The route dips slightly for the next mile where it crosses Onstott Creek, then winging to the west along the north side of Santa Rosa mountain with big pines above and an occasional oak-bordered streams crossing the road and an increasing view of the whole length of Palm Canyon with the desert and San Gorgonio mountain in the distant, and looking backward across the whole west slope of Pinon Flats, Deep Canyon and Sheep mountain appear again with Martinez mountain beyond.

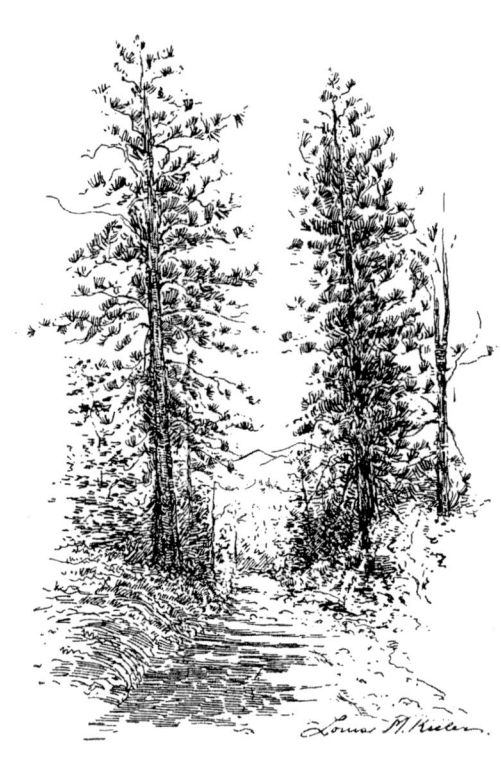

The road will then cross Vandeventer Flat at an elevation of 4,550 feet – a beautiful mountain meadow with streams and groups of oak and willow. This is part of the Santa Rosa Indian Reservation.

A little further west the route goes over the pass a little less than 5,000 feet high to the south end of Hemet valley, which runs northwest to the Hemet reservoir. Just west of this pass the road forks – the west branch going to Temecula, and the north branch on through this beautiful valley with extensive meadows, tall pines, bordering mountains and beautiful San Jacinto mountain straight ahead to Keen Camp, Idyllwild, Hemet, San Jacinto, and Banning.

This road is a necessity to the folks of Coachilla valley. They must have the quick way to get relief from the summer heat.

All the rest of Riverside county will benefit from this road.

Riverside county people will be spending their vacation money in Riverside county mountain resorts and thousands of acres of Riverside county territory will be made accessible. This route has the advantage over other possible routes in that it is an all-year round route, serving the great majority of the people. It is primarily a utility road, but of almost equal importance as a scenic route and will do a great deal to build Riverside county communities.

Appendix I

Pinon Pines Route for Mountain Highway Favored by Fulmor
County Surveyor Submits Preliminary Surveys of Three Possible Routes With Estimates of Cost

(Reported by Riverside Press, Reprinted in the Indio Date Palm, March 28, 1930)

R I V E R S I D E, March 1 8.— Report of County Surveyor A. C. Fulmor on proposed routes for the desert-to-mountain highway, presented to the supervisors late yesterday afternoon, recommends the adoption of the Pinon Pines route.

In his investigation and preliminary survey of the possible routes for the highway from the Keen Camp junction on the Idyllwild National Forest highway in the San Jacinto mountains to the Coachella valley, three different routes were investigated, says Fulmor.

These were the Palm canyon route, the Pinon Pines route and the West Fork of Palm canyon route. All begin at the same point in the mountains. The two Palm canyon routes reach the Coachella valley one mile south of Palm Springs, at the Palm Springs-Indio highway. The Pinon Pines route reaches the valley 12 miles west of Indio.

Estimated construction costs of the three routes were given by the surveyor as follows: Pinon Pines route, 37.3 miles in length, $361,900;. Palm canyon route, 38 miles in length, $504,600; West Fork of Palm canyon, 34 to 37 miles in length, $1,000,000 or $900,000.

In summarizing favorable conditions on the Pinon Pines route, the report says:

"The shortest route from the Coachella, Palo Verde and Imperial valleys. The cheapest route to build; can he finished by the present county equipment one year sooner than the Palm canyon route. A valley location for nearly one-half its length making for a fast and safe driving route. Opens a large area in the Hemet valley, Van Deventer Flat and Santa Rosa mountains to recreational use, not now served by a good road. Makes Pinon Flat area accessible,

Pinyon Flats with Sugarloaf Mountin in the distance, 1929
(Wieslander Vegetation Type Mapping Collection, courtesy of the Marian Koshland Bioscience and Natural Resources Library, University of California, Berkeley, www.lib.berkeley.edu/BIOS/vtm).

which has a summer climate in temperature about like the Hemet and San Jacinto area. Will make future additions to San Jacinto park accessible. A scenic route, groves of native palms, and tremendous canyons. Low elevation of summits crossed. Snow rarely lies on the ground.

The people from the Coachella valley will undoubtedly use this road during the summer season more than those from any other section. With an increased water supply from the Colorado river, the population of the valley will increase greatly. Pinon Flat, Santa Rosa mountain, Van de Venter Flat and the Hemet valley and Idyllwild, area are the nearest mountains to which the people of the Coachella Valley can go to get relief from the summer heat. This route offers these people the shortest distance route to the mountains, and one that will save them considerable time in getting to a cooler climate."

"This route will, I believe. be of more service to a greater number of taxpayers of Riverside county than any other route proposed. I recommend the adoption of the Pinon Pines route."

Gives Conditions

In the general summing up of his voluminous report, County Surveyor Fulmor says:

"Grade and alignment are satisfactory on both the Pinon Pines and Palm canyon routes. The ruling grade on each is 5 per cent with a maximum of 6 per cent. The Pinon Pines route has a slightly better alignment—longer tangents and fewer minimum radius curves.

West Fork Palm canyon route, favorable condition: The route over the San Jacinto mountains via the west fork of Palm canyon would be the shortest route to the Palm Springs area. It is admittedly a very scenic route; and would undoubtedly be used by a large number of tourists visiting Palm canyon who would return to Los Angeles and the coast via this route.

Unfavorable conditions; People from the lower end of the Coachella valley who might use this route to the Idyllwild area would have to travel 14 miles farther per round trip, then via the Pinon Pines route. It will open up comparatively little new area to recreational use. Its greater cost and length of time it will take to build as compared to other routes. Cost of snow removal during winter season.

Palm Canyon route, favorable conditions: Shortest route from the Palm Springs area, opens a large area in the Hemet valley, Van Deventer Flats and Santa Rosa mountains to recreational use not now served by a good road. A valley location for nearly one-half of its length; a fast and safe driving route; low elevation of summits crossed; snow will seldom lay on the ground. Will make new views of Palm canyon accessible and increase its fame. More tourists would probably use this route than any other, especially during the winter season.

Unfavorable conditions: People from the lower end of the Coachella valley, Palo Verde and the Imperial valley who might use this route to Idyllwild and Keen Camp area would have to travel 21.6 miles farther per round trip than via the Pinon Pines route. Greater cost and greater length of time to construct than the Pinon Pines route."

No unfavorable conditions were outlined as to the Pinon Pines route by Fulmor.

Details of Route

Concerning the West Fork route, the cost of which apparently would be prohibitive, the report outlines the route as an extremely scenic one, reaching an elevation as high as 6000 feet,

"The steep side slopes, narrow ridges and deep canyon over which a large portion of this route would be located, make the excavation extremely heavy and costly," says the report.

In detailing Pinon Pines and Palm canyon routes, it is shown that they are identical for the 16.4 miles from the Idyllwild National Forest highway at the Keen Camp junction, to Van Deventer Flats. This portion of the road is via Herkey creek, around the head of the Hemet reservoir or lake, up the pine-clad Hemet valley, to the divide between the watersheds of Palm canyon and the south fork of the San Jacinto river, at the west boundary of the Santa Rosa Indian reservation. The distance to this point 'is 14 miles. From the divide the location extends easterly on a descending 5 per cent grade to Van Deventer Flats. This point is the junction of the Palm canyon and Pinon Pines routes.

View up West Fork of Palm Canyon, 1929
(Wieslander Vegetation Type Mapping Collection, courtesy of the Marian Koshland Bioscience and Natural Resources Library, University of California, Berkeley, www.lib.berkeley.edu/BIOS/vtm).

Palm Canyon from the West Fork trail

Routes Diverge

The Pinon Pines route turns to the east from this point and follows along the north slope of the Santa Rosa mountain, crossing the divide between Onstott and Deep canyons and going thence around the south side of Sugar Loaf mountain, thence northeasterly to Black hill, and passing around the east flank of that mountain and down the divide between Carrizo and Deep canyons.

Distance has to be developed in this section to overcome the difference in elevation of the steep drop to the floor of the valley. The location reaches the wash of Dead Indian creek and continues to the paved highway between Indio and Palm Springs.

An alternate route between Onstott creek and Black Hill was surveyed, passing over route on which a road can be more cheaply constructed, but would be one and one-half miles longer. Other alternates along the route are suggested in the survey report, particularly to allow the road to pass along the brink of Deep canyon. "Should a road be built on this location, Deep canyon will become famous as one of the most scenic points of the southwest," says Fulmor. The Salton sea is visible from this route.

"The greater portion of both the Pinon Pines and the Palm canyon routes passes over country on which a high type of road can be located and built at a small cost per mile," he says. "On steep side slopes broken by deep ravines, a few curves of a minimum radius of 200 feet have been used to reduce the cost of construction. The radius of these curves can be increased except in a few cases by increasing the excavation. A type of alignment that would meet with the approval of state and federal agencies has been used with the purpose that at some future time this road might become a part of the National Forest highway system."

Appendix J

Celebration of Opening of the Pines-to-Palms Highway

Program

(Reprinted in the Indio Date Palm, *June 17, 1932)*

Saturday

    8:00 A. M. – Cutting ribbon which will open road on this side of the mountain.

    11:00 A. M. – Celebration starts officially at Keen Camp. Introduction of prominent guests and short talks.

    12:00 P. M. – Big Free Barbecue.

    The afternoon will be spent in visiting and trips over the new road

    8:00 P. M. – Dance at Tahquitz Lodge

Sunday

    11:00 A. M. – Devotional serives at Keen Camp in charge of Rev. Stanley N. Bond with music by Mrs. Bond and choir of Christian Church

    Afternoon – Informal program by local talent.

The contractors have agreed to keep the road unobstructed from 8 to 10 a. m. and from 4 to 6 p. m. on both Saturday and Sunday. At other times visitors may be delayed slightly.

Appendix K

Fitting Remarks by Chairman B. H. Hayes

(Maj. Bartlett Hayes' speech at the opening ceremonies of the Pines-to-Palms Highway, as reproduced in the Indio Date Palm, *June 24, 1932)*

Friends: We are gathered together here to greet one another and to express our sense of great happiness that one more highway, connecting the Coast region with the Desert, is near completion.

You who live on the west slope of the San Jacinto range will now have safe and easy access over these magnificent mountains, through beautiful virgin timber, to the Desert section of the Coachella Valley. We salute you. Do be neighborly!

The happy traveler, seeking quiet, rest and vistas of natural beauty, will be enchanted by the rapid change in physical transformation of Mother Earth in passing over this Highway from West to East, or East to West. Looking down from these mountain heights to the East the realm of the Desert will unfold itself.

The Desert – brimming over with enchantment; a lure to lovers of nature.

The Desert – beautifully depicted by that lawyer-poet, Bruce McDaniel, warning all trespassers:

"Who seeks my gold, finds Death,
Who comes to me with faith and open heart
Yield I my soul."

And you who live in the Desert. What does this day mean to you? Long years you have endured the cruel heat of a clear summer sky, determined to conquer an arid country and transform it into production! At night, still sweltering in a suffocating atmosphere, you have looked longingly towards those mountains. You have craved some quick passage to the cool, sweet air of higher altitudes where quiet, healthful sleep might be obtained!

Rejoice! Your wish is about to be consummated.

Let me briefly give credit for the conception and completion of this wonderful highway to those to whom credit is due.

First to J. Win. Wilson, Lorenzo D. Mallory and Wilson Howell, the men who conceived the possibilities of a road.

Bartlett Hayes, c. 1917
(Photo courtesy Dorothy Hayes)

Mallory and Wilson, long residents of the valley, were the first on the scene. They persistently and courageously traversed the mountains on both sides of the valley, seeking water holes and an easy grade to the heights above and beyond. Careful exploration proved that the San Jacinto range held forth the greatest and most desirable possibilities.

Then appeared Wilson Howell. He took up the task that Mallory had to abandon because of illness.

For two or three years these two men, Win Wilson and Wilson Howell, dogged in their determination to find a route, persistent – almost to the point of exasperation – in trying to make friends see the feasibility of their plan, scoured the mountains from the Valley to Keen camp, over and over again.

Encouragement first came to these pioneers from Nash-Boulden, at that time United States Supervisor of the Cleveland and San Bernardino National Forests. Friends in the valley suddenly saw the practicability of the vision themselves, and a conference was held with the Honorable Board of Supervisors of Riverside county. As a result of this conference County Engineer Fulmor and Ed Bunker made a reconnaissance of the proposed road and their investigation proved the feasibility of the plan and added further enthusiasm to the movement. Letters and words of encouragement, promising assistance, began to pour in from Palo Verde Valley, San Diego county, Imperial county, and even Arizona.

Confident in the righteousness of their cause, meetings were held in the Valley and petitions circulated. As a result, I believe I am correct in saying, that for the first time in the history of any public endeavor in the Valley, every religious, fraternal and social organization and every individual that could be contacted, unanimously and enthusiastically supported a movement to request the Honorable Board of Supervisors to construct the road. Final action was taken by the board at a meeting held July 22, 1930, and a vote was passed duly authorizing the construction of the road within the county boundaries.

To the Honorable Board of Supervisors we all owe our deepest gratitude. In times of elation or depression all public administrative bodies are subject to demands for expenditures of public funds. These demands come from all conceivable sources, public and private, but invariably, thank God, those propositions that are pertinent, real, and of necessity, win out.

Mr. Jamison, to you and to your fellow members of the board of supervisors the people of Coachella valley extend their humble but hearty thanks for the action you took on July 22, 1930. You realized that the necessity of providing a safe and speedy access into higher altitudes, during the heat of summer months, was essential to the public health and welfare of the people of Coachella valley. Once the engineers proved that a road was feasible, both practically and from a standpoint of reasonable cost, your decision was made. I am confident that time will prove the wisdom of that decision.

Next in the procession of helpful co-operation came the activities and support of the United States Department of Forestry and the United Sates Bureau of Public Roads. Their assistance was absolutely essential in order to build the road through public domain.

To the heads of these different Departments, to their surveyors, engineers, and other employees, who labored ceaselessly to perfect the final plans and construction plans, we extend heartfelt thanks and warm congratulations for the magnificent manner in which the road has been built.

To the contractors, Messrs. Frank E. Cuffe and Leo Honek, and to their sturdy, fearless employees who performed the actual work of construction, all honor, all praise, and heartiest thanks are due.

Work on the eastern end of the road was started November 15, 1931. Seven months later, almost to a day, we have been privileged to emerge from the Desert and come over these rugged mountains to this spot. Time and distance has been shattered. In this successful endeavor of Man to overcome all obstacles of nature, masses of rock have been torn asunder and moved to make "cut and fill." Direction and care have been so exercised that not a single human life has been sacrificed and loss of equipment by accident has been reduced to a minimum. This is, indeed, a marvelous piece of work.

Last, but by no means least, come our friends (and I use that term advisedly) the Santa Rosa tribe of Indians.

All the splendid plans of the board of supervisors and the United States Government would have proven futile had not active support and co-operation been granted by these Indians. They gave our duly constituted authorities a right of way across the Indian Reservation at Van Der Venter Flats that made possible the connection of the east and west ends of the road.

Their property is Private not Public property. Their growth of Live Oak and other trees are majestic. They have granted us the right to pass through this Reservation, but let us not forget that we, one and all, must guard their property against trespass, against fire, against any other destructive act perpetrated through careless thought or otherwise. We salute these Indian friends and, with gratitude, the citizens of Coachella valley pledge them loyal support.

I am through with my brief sketch of this history leading up to the construction of this road. If I have omitted mention of some individual to whom mention and thanks are due, please lay that act to the vagaries of my mind and not to my heart. I, personally, am so excited over the fact that this road is near final completion that I simply cannot believe it to be true. I am wandering in fairyland.

Before closing, however, I desire to leave one through with you. For some reason or other the name "Pines-to-Palms" has been attached to his road. No longer do we hear of "Dead Indian Trail" or "Pinon Pines" road.

I am one of those who always believes in bestowing honor and recognition on all those citizens who accomplish some outstanding act for the good of the community "outside the line of duty."

Two men, Win Wilson and Wilson Howell, conceived the idea of this road and fostered it. To their everlasting credit let it be said that their every act and thought in the movement has been to advance the health and welfare of the people of Coachella valley. I, therefore, am bold enough to suggest, before it is too late, that these two Wilsons be honored and that thereafter the name of this road be changed from Pines-to-Palms to Wilson Highway.

Appendix L

New Highway Over San Jacinto Mountain Area
Pines-to-Palms Road Joins Virgin
Forest and Coachella Desert by
Direct Easy Route

By Lynn L. Rogers
(*Los Angeles* Times, *October 9, 1932*)

Within easy reach by a day's drive, and offering many interesting and varied scenic wonders is the trip to Coachella Valley via the recently developed Pines-to-Palms Highway. Motorists seeking new territory to invade and yearning for the thrill of formerly inaccessible mountain scenery will find this trip a rare treat.

Not only does this route open up a vast new area to motor travel but it now enables the hunter to gain access by automobile to some of the best deer country in the Southland.

Residents of Coachella Valley during the summer are enabled to commute daily to the higher altitudes where cool, refreshing sleep may be enjoyed after a high daytime summer temperature.

ROAD SECTION UNIQUE

This interesting new section of road is unique; it carries the motorists from an approximate altitude of one mile to below sea level in less than two hours' driving. There is approximately thirty-seven miles of the new portion of the road which makes the direct connection between Hemet and Indio. This mileage is found between Idyllwild and the Palm Springs cut-off from Highway 99.

Ten miles of the new road was built by the United States Forest Service and twenty-seven miles by the county of Riverside.

The road is constructed of native material, principally decomposed granite, and is a remarkabley fine piece of engineering. Almost $500,000 has been expended, and eventually it is planned to hard surface the entire distance, which will afford a high-grade highway between Hemet and Indio.

It was to this section that the Times scout car . . . headed last week. Leaving Los Angeles early in the morning fog the scout car sped out Valley Boulevard through Riverside and Perris to Hemet. Not until leaving Riverside did the gray mist lift. Turning east at Hemet we headed the car toward Idyllwild.

TO BE FINISHED SOON

Near the foot of the grade we passed a crew of men engaged in repairing the highway, and upon investigation were informed that the road was being filled in and leveled off as far as Idyllwild and would be completed within the week.

Arriving at Idyllwild we enjoyed a late breakfast with Mr. Emerson, general manager of the resort. After a short stay we returned to the junction of the Idyllwild road, near Tahquitz Lodge where the new Pines-to-Palms highway road begins. Heading toward Indio through a wide mountain valley fringed with tall pines at an elevation of 5000 feet, we crossed Herkey Creek with its public camp grounds past Hemet Lake and Garner ranch where huge black oaks and willows line Omstott Creek, and blossoming red shank grows tall and thick beside the road.

DESERT DOMAIN UNFOLDS

As we neared Pinyon Flat the desert domain unfolded itself before our eyes. Here a halt was made, we climbed out of the car and looking back across the shoulders of the majestic peak of San Jacinto, towering above Tahquitz peak, we were held spellbound by its sheer beauty. San Jacinto has an elevation of over 10,800 feet, and is the second largest mountain peak in Southern California.

Entering the car again we traveled down through Dead Indian Canyon into the Santa Rosa foothills. There we found the lower slopes as barren and forbidding as desert can be. One thing that makes this trip interesting after leaving the mountain pines is the variety of desert growth. Many species of desert sage and greasewood dot the sun-baked hills; several varieties of cactus, flaming Ocotillo, Cholla, Barrel Cactus and even the Maguay, which is rarely found on our local desert help to complete the desert gardens. A short distance and we reached the end of the new road eleven miles from Indio.

The last four miles of the new Pines-to-Palms road is paved and in excellent condition; the balance is fair, although a bit rough on account of the heavy travel of sight-seers and Coachella Valley residents who have gone over the road since its opening to traffic last August. Driving on to Indio we inspected several of the large date farms for which this section is famous, and after lunch headed the car toward Palm Springs, making stops at Palm, Tahquitz and Andreas canyons.

The return trip from Palm Springs was made via Banning, Beaumont, Redlands and San Bernardino . . . covering exactly 298 miles for the entire trip.

Appendix M

Where (and What) the Heck was Ribbonwood?

(Article written by the author in 2006)

Ribbonwood was the brainchild of Wilson Stout Howell Jr. If that name sounds somewhat familiar, it's because his father Wilson Howell was one of the top scientists working with Thomas Edison at his Menlo Park facility. The contributions of Howell Sr. were numerous, and he was able to amass no small amount of money in his later years.

Wilson Jr. was born in New Jersey on July 9, 1888, one of three children of Wilson Sr. and his wife Emma. As a young man, Wilson Jr. stood nearby to see some of the many experimental flights of the Wright brothers.[1] This early fascination with airplanes led him to study mechanics and some engineering, and he spent the years during World War I as a designer and inspector in an aircraft factory.[2] After the war, he decided to come west for health reasons. In 1919, Howell came to Indio and began operating a ranch south of that town.[3] The ranch he took over already had 2½ acres set out to Marsh seedless grapefruit, which did well in the Coachella Valley sun and even better with Howell's care. Howell soon started a mail-order business selling the fruit, which he picked only when ripe and shipped in quarter boxes.[4] This became quite popular, and he had a large amount of trade for one person.

Howell slowly improved his land, leveling it by hand and planting other fruits such as figs, table grapes, and Deglet Noor dates. The dates apparently were the fruit he thought would ultimately do the best, since he indicated that the trees would eventually be the dominant crop on his ranch.[5]

However, after nearly ten years of work in Indio, he found that both the heat of the low desert and the long hours of work it took to make his ranch a success were taking a toll on his health. Although he liked the area, he began looking for a location that was out of the intense heat, but still in the same vicinity. He soon turned his attention to the Santa Rosa Mountains to the west and began looking for a place that was still within view of the desert, but would not be so hot. He found such a location, and began a most interesting, but overlooked, chapter in Riverside County's history.

The land that Howell found was situated at the base of Santa Rosa Mountain and the head of Palm Canyon. It was at the crossroads of several existing trails and was dotted with springs. Before the turn of the century, it had been an Indian rancheria known as *Gabelon*. Beginning in the 1890s, when cattlemen from the desert and the Cahuilla Valley area began driving cattle to market through there, it was known as Brush Corral. It became a way-stop for cattle drives due to the abundance of water and for the corrals that were built around the springs.[6] By the time Howell became interested in the property, it was just one more set of parcels the Southern Pacific Railroad was trying to sell from their massive land subsidy.

Wilson Howell, 1944
(Photo courtesy Desert Magazine)

Howell fell in love with the area, and saw much potential in it. He had very little cash to make a purchase, though, so at first he tried to form a cooperative (they were later called communes) with some friends and neighbors. That idea quickly fell through, so Howell appealed to his father, who by now was living in Escondido, for the money. Howell Sr. obliged, and Howell Jr. subsequently purchased three full sections of land (1916.64 acres total - Sections 7, 17, and 21 of Township 7 South, Range 5 East) from the Southern Pacific Railroad, which had been granted the land back in the 1870s when it built through the Coachella Valley.[7]

When Wilson Howell purchased his property and moved onto it, his intention was to farm the land just as he had previously done in the desert. The new lands, though, offered many challenges that awaited him. First of all, he noticed that during rainstorms, large torrents of water would flow off the hills carrying topsoil and rocks off the property. Howell saw this as a waste, and decided to start damming the many rivulets that dotted his land. This began what would become an obsession to keep the water that fell on his property on his property. He built check dams out of masonry, concrete, wood, brush, rock, and dirt across the many depressions on the site. These check dams served to hold water and eroded topsoil and keep it on the property. Then, one of two things would happen to the water. In most instances, it was allowed to percolate back into the soil and remain underground until it could be pumped from one of the many springs that existed on site. In the larger culverts, however, he constructed a series of pipes that led to reservoirs that in turn acted as catch basins for water that would be available for immediate use. These reservoirs doubled as swimming holes for children in the area. In 1954, *Westways* Magazine writer Vernon Luckock asked Howell just how many dams he had constructed throughout the years. Howell proudly told him that "I guess I've built at least 4,500 of them, all told . . . About 1,500 of them are major dams, the rest just little ones."[8] Howell's system worked well, and it was remembered that he always had an abundance of water, no matter what the season.[9]

Once Howell worked out the details of how to furnish his property with enough water, he turned to the issue of raising crops. The northwestern portion of his property was fairly flat, and he quickly started to experiment with various orchards. Over the years, he planted orchards of apples, peaches, pears and other fruits, and had a large garden where he was able to grow most of the food he needed. Wilson Howell was described as an organic farmer long before the term had come into vogue.[10] After leveling an area for planting, he would "feed" the soil by layering leaves, brush trimmings, and manure on it and leaving it to decompose. He continued this practice throughout the years, and was able to boast of some of the biggest and best produce anywhere. Long-time area resident Harry Quinn remembers riding with Howell in his old truck (in which a passenger could spread his feet and watch the highway go by underneath) to pick up fallen oak leaves from various places around the area for his compost heaps.[11] "Feeding" the soil in this way helped in two ways

- it added organic materials to what is generally considered a rather sandy, mineral-rich soil, and it helped to retain the precious water that Howell delivered via his intricate network.

Once Howell began to improve his land, which in turn allowed him to improve himself outside the strong desert heat, Howell set out to improve his property and make his own "Garden of Eden" - one that many others could enjoy too. He believed that the area would make an ideal get-away place for people wanting to relax in a better climate. There was one small problem though - access. Although the property was located on old trails, there was no good road leading to his place,[12] and the closest true road ended at the Idyllwild Junction/ Keen Camp area (now Mountain Center) 12 miles to the north. To alleviate this problem, Howell joined the growing campaign led by Indio *Date Palm* editor J. Winn Wilson to have a new access road built between Idyllwild and the Coachella Valley. This campaign resulted in the construction of the much-advertised Pines-to-Palms Highway, which was opened in June 1932. This new access road stretched from Idyllwild southeast through Wilson Howell's property, through Pinyon Flats, along Deep Canyon, and eventually connected to the Coachella Valley on the Indio Highway (today's Highway 111) at a point that in later years would become Palm Desert.[13]

With the opening of this new highway came Howell's most notable effort. Taking his cue from the many people who for centuries had settled along old roads and trails and established roadside stations, Wilson Howell cleared an area abutting the highway and constructed a brush ramada that became a store. He named his place Ribbonwood after the predominant vegetation cover there (*Adenostoma sparsifolium* - more commonly called Redshanks). At his brush store, Howell sold produce from his farm, postcards, drinks, and handicrafts that he had fashioned out of the ribbonwood, chamise, and many other woody materials he had cleared from his property.[14]

After completion of the store, Howell built a few more brush ramadas that served as covered picnic areas for people passing through. In two of these ramadas, he constructed rock fireplaces with chimneys so that picnickers could avail themselves of a fire for heat or a barbeque. However, Howell was not content to just run a store and picnic area. Because the move to the mountains had cured his ill health, he believed that others would follow him for the same

"RIBBONWOOD" ON THE PALMS TO PINES HIGHWAY, CALIFORNIA
WILSON'S HQ GALLERY
RIBBONWOOD VIA IDYLLWILD CAMP CALIF.

In 1944, Mabel Wilton, a free-lance writer for Desert Magazine, visited Ribbonwood and asked Howell about his plans. It apparently pleased him that someone was interested, and he indicated that:

> I am trying to make this place into a sort of community rest center, or in other words a rest resort for people in ill health. I want to make it into a place that is entirely different from the general run of health resorts. A quiet, peaceful place with all the comforts of home, yet retaining as much of the natural scenery and atmosphere as possible. Something entirely rustic from beginning to end where sick people can come for the rest and relaxation they so badly need. I would prefer to make it into a place where artists, writers, scholars and scientists, who are badly in need of just such an environment, can come and forget their work for a brief spell, yet at the same time they can be surrounded by a beautiful natural setting. Instead of just the two cabins I have here now, I have visions of a group of log cabins up here on the top of this mountain, with lots of roads and trails leading to the most scenic spots. There could be a tennis court and a swimming pool, horseback riding, hiking and all kinds of sports. There are all sorts of hideaway places here among these rocks and it's an ideal place to come to get away from the hubub of city life.[17]

Throughout the 1940s and 1950s, Howell continued to farm, cater to tourists and travelers at Ribbonwood, and enjoy his holdings in the Santa Rosa Mountains. The year 1940 saw a major fire sweep through the area, taking Howell's house and the main ramada at Ribbonwood. But he rebuilt, and continued his efforts. Although he suffered a major heart attack around 1950, which left him unable to do heavy work, Howell continued to maintain his site and provide produce to Idyllwild and some of the resorts that were springing up in the desert.[18]

By the early 1960s, Howell had decided to move on. He was in his 70s, and the upkeep on his massive project was getting to be too much for the one man.[19] He placed the property on the market, and in February 1964, found a buyer in William and Gloria Newell.

reason. So, above the Ribbonwood highway turnout, he built picnic areas throughout his property and cleared approximately ten miles of roads and trails so visitors could enjoy them.[15]

To further welcome people to his "Garden of Eden," Howell conceived of the idea of building small rental cabins. Apparently, though, Howell was not much of a builder, because on November 1, 1935, he entered into an agreement with an H. R. Van Horn of Loma Linda to build "neat rustic cabins" at Ribbonwood. Van Horn was to receive $.85 for each night a cabin was rented, with the option that Howell could purchase the cabins after five years.[16] Van Horn built 6-8 cabins, which became quite popular. With these and many other improvements, Ribbonwood became a well-known way-station on the Pines-to-Palms Highway.

In order to boost the number of visitors to his Ribbonwood "resort," Howell approached owners of some of the well-known hotels in Palm Springs. Because many of the visitors were sometimes eager to see different scenery, or escape some of the warmer days, excursions began to be run from Palm Springs to Ribbonwood. On March 24, 1935, the Los Angeles *Times* indicated that guests of the El Mirador Hotel in Palm Springs had spent mid-day at Ribbonwood with a picnic lunch and a tour along the Pines-to-Palms Highway. Similarly, the famed Desert Inn maintained an outdoor grill area at Ribbonwood, to which they would take guests for similar outings.

The Desert Inn's retreat at Ribbonwood, 1930s

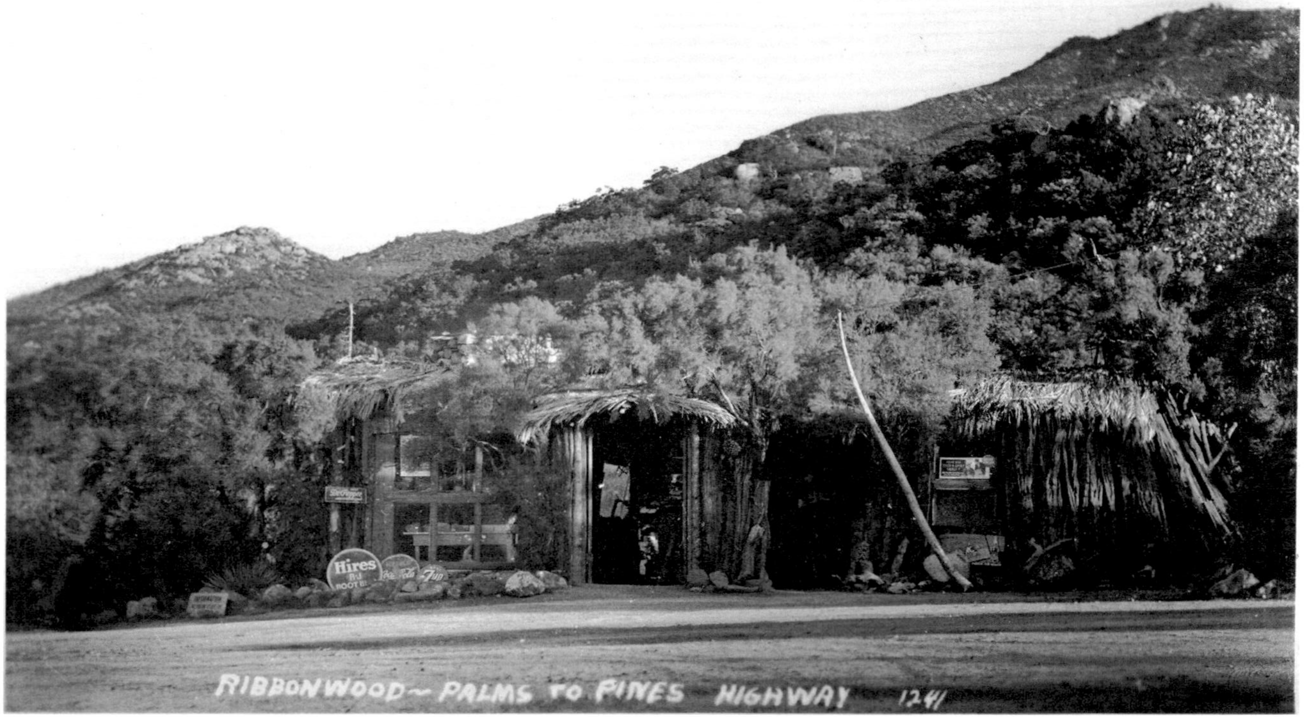
Hires
ROOT BEER
7up
RIBBONWOOD ~ PALMS TO PINES HIGHWAY 1241

The Newells were both interested in real estate and development, although they had come from differing careers - he had been a miner and aircraft part manufacturer, and she a singer with such bands as Tommy Dorsey's and Joe Venuti's. The Newells purchased all 1916 acres of Howell's property, and began a massive development scheme called Spring Crest, which is the name by which Ribbonwood is known today. Spring Crest was touted as the newest city in the desert. It was going to be a haven for winter recreation and was going to offer homesites on 1-acre lots. Planned within Spring Crest was a ski lodge (it was said that there would be at least 100 days per year of snow!), riding and hiking trails, picnic areas, and a golf course. In addition, the various streams would be dammed and the resulting reservoirs stocked with trout for fishermen.[20]

Needless to say, in looking at Spring Crest today, none of the proposed amenities took shape. While several of the 1,916 acres were divided into 1-acre parcels, and roads were built, Spring Crest today can boast of only a few houses and none of the sporting centers originally proposed by the Newells. The only non-residential improvements that can be readily identified today include an abandoned gas station along Highway 74 (which was supposed to be a gas station, market, and restaurant), and a water tank belonging to the Spring Crest Water and Power Company. Nothing remains of Howell's brush structures or his cabins, which isn't surprising. However, a quick reconnaissance around the old Ribbonwood area showed that his main reservoir is still recognizable, as are a number of the check dams, especially those on the north side of Highway 74. Those that remain have long since silted over, and resemble steps more than actual dams.

Wilson Howell and the development of Ribbonwood remind us of the days when rugged individualists could and would purchase property for themselves and make it into a unique place that had a story of its own. Like Harry Oliver in 1000 Palms, or "Desert" Steve Ragsdale in Desert Center, Wilson Howell Jr. became a fixture for many years along a road that was advertised far and wide. Although he is probably one of the least remembered of the group that inhabited Riverside County, Howell's touch definitely added a unique story, long untold, in the history of our area.

Sidelight

A side chapter to the story of Wilson Howell and Ribbonwood is that of Louise Teagarden. Louise Teagarden was a nurse who lived in the Coachella Valley. Apparently, she was a bit of a loner, and was the black sheep of her family. Family members expected her to take care of their ailing mother because she was unmarried and a nurse. Over the course of several years, when she'd had all she could take, she would pack up her backpack and hike up to Ribbonwood, where she would stay either in the open or in a small ante room in Howell's cabin that was originally designed to be a firewood storage room. For several days or sometimes weeks, Teagarden would hike around the area, enjoying the solitude, and mapping every little spring, seep, or other source of water in the area, keeping the information on folded USGS quadrangle sheets. Louise used Ribbonwood as her "get-away" place at least from the mid-1940s and throughout the 1950s. However, in December 1959, Louise left Ribbonwood in a car, bound for Hemet to do some shopping - and never returned. Weeks later, her car was found abandoned, with the radiator cap on the seat (Howell had instructed her that if she was going to leave a car for a while, and there was a danger of freezing, to drain the radiator and put the cap on the seat as a reminder). She never returned to either her home or Ribbonwood, and for over 30 years her disappearance remained a mystery. It was not until 1991 when a hiker found the remains of Louise Teagarden far up in Palm Canyon. Apparently she had stopped to hike, fell, and died where she enjoyed spending time - in the San Jacinto/Santa Rosa Mountains area.[21]

l to r - Harry Caldwell, Louise Teagarden, Harry Quinn, and unidentified woman at Ribbonwood, c. 1947
(Photo courtesy Harry Quinn)

Norton Allen map showing route to Ribbonwood, 1944 (Photo courtesy Desert Magazine)

Notes

1. Los Angeles *Times*, September 13, 1953.
2. Los Angeles *Times*, February 20, 1927.
3. Although most accounts indicate that the ranch in Indio was his, no evidence that he purchased the land could be found in the official records of Riverside County.
4. Los Angeles *Times,* February 20, 1927.
5. *Ibid.*
6. Clarence Contreras, early settler and cattleman, as quoted in Quinn, Harry. "Mr. Wilson Howell and His Ribbonwood Mountain Home." Coachella Valley Archaeological Society Occasional Papers, No. 1; January 1997, pp. 35-38.
7. Riverside County Deed Book 307, pp. 423-424, December 2, 1936. It was often the case that the deed was recorded well after the actual sale. This could have been an administrative lag on the part of the Southern Pacific, or it could have been simply a way of ensuring that Howell paid all of the $5,099 that was owed before he received title.
8. Luckock, Vernon O. "He Face-Lifted a Mountain." Westways Magazine, October, 1954, pp. 8-9.
9. Quinn, Harry. Personal communication with the author, June 16, 2006.
10. Quinn, Harry. Personal communication with the author, June 16, 2006.
11. Quinn, Harry. Personal communication with the author, June 16, 2006.
12. An interesting legend sprang up regarding Howell and access to his property. Howell had a Model T Ford that he drove from Ribbonwood through Pinyon Flats and along Deep Canyon. He then stashed it when he could travel no farther, and hike down into the valley and eventually the 15 miles to Indio. Later, he purchased another Model T to shuttle him between Indio and the side of the mountain. The legend soon grew that Howell had "discovered" a road up to the mountains, when in fact he was using two cars and stashing them when he had to get out and hike!
13. One other familiar landmark in the area came about due to the construction of the highway - Hurkey Creek Park, which still caters to campers some 75 years later.

14. Some of the items included rings made from ribbonwood, charms, and decorative nic-knacks.

15. According to most accounts, Howell cleared the roads by hand, first clearing the brush then leveling the underlying ground with his shovel and wheelbarrow.

16. Riverside County Deed Book 304, pp. 491-492, November 1, 1935.

17. Wilton, Mabel. "Paradise - Above the Palms." Desert Magazine, Palm Desert, California: July 1944, pp. 4-7.

18. Luckock, Vernon O. "He Face-Lifted a Mountain." Westways Magazine, October, 1954, pp. 8-9.

19. Wilson Howell died October 5, 1967.

20. "Spring Crest Offers Buyers Choice of Climate." Los Angeles *Times*, January 26, 1966.

21. Quinn, Harry. Personal communication with the author, June 16, 2006.

One of Wilson Howell's check dams today

Bibliography

California Highway Commission. *Investigation and Report of Toll Bridges in the State of California*. California Highway Commission, Sacramento, California: 1929.

Cavanaugh, Lucille (daughter of Charlie and Opelia Tune). Personal communication with the author, January 16, 2012.

Conlin, Mike. "Historic Jefferson Highway and the Links Between Winnipeg, Canada and New Orleans, Louisiana." http://maps.bc.ca/jeffhwy/index2.htm.

Cuffe, Marshal (son of contractor Frank Cuffe). Personal communication with the author, December 2, 2011.

Davis, Richard Carter. "Wilderness, Politics, and Bureaucracy: Federal and State Policies in the Administration of San Jacinto Mountain, Southern California, 1920-1968." Ph.D. Dissertation, University of California, Riverside, Riverside, California: 1973.

Fitch, Robert. *Profile of a Century*. Riverside County Historical Commission Press, Riverside, California: 1993.

Fulmor, Alexander C. (Compiler). "Map of Riverside County California Showing Sections, Townships, Ranch Lines, and Topography." Published by Davidson and Fulmor, Riverside, California: 1929.

Fulmor, Alexander C. (Compiler) "Map of Riverside County California Showing Sections, Townships, Ranch Lines, and Topography." Published by Davidson and Fulmor, Riverside, California: 1936.

Gunther, Jane Davies. *Riverside County, California Place Names - Their Origins and Their Stories*. Rubidoux Printing Company, Riverside, California: 1984.

Hayes, Dorothy (daugther-in-law of Maj. Bartlett Hayes). Personal communication with the author, December 1, 2011.

Hemet *News*, various dates as cited in text.

Honek, Milton (son of contractor Leo Honek). Personal communication with the author, December 1, 2011.

Indio *Date Palm*, various dates as cited in text.

James, George Wharton. *The Wonders of the Colorado Desert*. Little, Brown, and Company, Boston, Massachusetts: 1906.

Law, George. "The 'Pines and Palm Trails' of Wonder." Los Angeles *Times*, October 3, 1920.

Lech, Steve. *Along the Old Roads - A History of the Portion of Southern California That Became Riverside County, 1772 - 1893.* Privately published by the author, Riverside, California: 2004.

Lech, Steve. *More Than a Place to Pitch a Tent – The Stories Behind Riverside County's Regional Parks.* Privately published by the author, Riverside, California: 2011.

Los Angeles *Times*, various dates as cited in text.

Quinn, Harry. "Mr. Wilson Howell and His Ribbonwood Mountain Home." Coachella Valley Archaeological Society Occasional Papers, No. 1, January, 1997: pp 35-38.

Quinn, Harry. Personal communication with the author, as cited in text.

Riverside County Board of Supervisors. Minutes. Various dates, as cited in text.

Riverside County Planning Department. "The 'Pines to Palms' Scenic Corridor - A Plan and Action Program to Preserve Our Beautiful San Jacinto-Santa Rosa Mountains." County of Riverside Planning Department, Riverside, California: December, 1969.

Riverside *Daily Press*, various dates as cited in text.

Riverside *Enterprise*, various dates as cited in text.

San Jacinto *Register*, various dates as cited in text.

Shumway, Nina Paul. *Your Desert and Mine.* Westernlore Press, Los Angeles, California: 1960.

Wild, Peter. *William Pester: The Hermit of Palm Springs.* The Shady Myrick Research Project, Johannesburg, California: 2008.

About the Author

Steve Lech is a researcher, author, and lecturer of the history of Riverside County, California. A native Riversider, his interest in local history dates back more than 35 years. He began working for Riverside County in 1986, and since that time has been exploring many aspects of the history of the county. One of the avenues on which his research took him was the fascinating story of how Riverside County came into existence both geographically and politically. This led to his first self-published book, *Along the Old Roads*, which has been described as the definitive history of Riverside County's settlement and formation. Other works include *Riverside in Vintage Postcards, Resorts of Riverside County, Riverside's Mission Inn* (co-authored with longtime friend and Jurupa-area historian Kim Jarrell Johnson), and *Riverside 1870-1940*, all of which were published by Arcadia Publishing. In 2011, Steve self-published his 6th book, this one entitled *More Than a Place to Pitch a Tent - The Stories Behind Riverside County's Regional Parks*.

Steve has been a docent with the Mission Inn Foundation for more than 20 years, and has been President of the Riverside Historical Society for several years. In 2008, he was awarded the Individual Achievement Award for Outstanding Contributions to Local History by the Riverside County Historical Commission, and in 2009 he was recognized by the City of Riverside's Cultural Heritage Board with an Individual Achievement Award for Outstanding Contributions to Local History.

Ocotillo and Agave in Bloom on the Pines to Palms Highway, near Palm Springs, California